CW00933156

What readers are saying

This sprightly, accessible biography rescues Hannah More from unde-
served neglect. In it, Mary Anne Phemister shows clearly why More's
remarkable life—as dramatist, educator, best-selling author, anti-slave
campaigner, and deeply Christian witness—can inspire believers today
almost as much as she did during her own lifetime.

> —**Mark Noll,** The Francis A. McAnaney Professor of History at University
> of Notre Dame; author of *The Rise of Evangelicalism: The Age of Edwards,
> Whitefield, and the Wesleys*

This lively and engaging work shows Hannah More's continuing rele-
vance to the modern world.

> —**Anne Stott**, author of *Hannah More: The First Victorian*

With her book *Hannah More: The Artist as Reformer,* Mary Anne Phemister provides an engaging look at a neglected woman writer who certainly deserves more of our attention today. By combining discussions of
Hannah More's influence and stories of her life with visual images of the
places lived and visited, Phemister gives her readers a glimpse into the
world that Hannah More inhabited and tried to transform for the better.

> —**Christine A. Colón,** associate professor of English at Wheaton College;
> author of *Joanna Baillie and the Art of Moral Influence*

HANNAH MORE

The
Artist
as
Reformer

MARY ANNE PHEMISTER

for Mark
Be Inspired

Ps. 46: 1, 2

Mary Anne Phemister

DeepRiver
B O O K S

Also by Mary Anne Phemister

32 Wheaton Notables: Their Stories and Where They Lived

Mere Christians: Inspiring Stories of Encounters with C. S. Lewis
with Andrew Lazo, co-editor

Lessons From a Broken Chopstick: A Memoir of a Peculiar Childhood

Hannah More, The Artist as Reformer

© 2014 Mary Anne Phemister

All Scripture quotations are taken from the Holy Bible, King James Version. Public domain

Published by
Deep River Books
Sisters, Oregon
www.deepriverbooks.com

ISBN-13: 9781940269313
ISBN-10:1940269318

Library of Congress: 2014952806
Printed in the USA

Design by Robin Black, www.InspirioDesign.com.

To Bill
without whose love,
encouragement, and support
this book
would never have been completed.

CONTENTS

The term *evangelical* is used in many ways throughout the world. For this book, I will use the descriptives summarized by noted church historian David Bebbington. His four key ingredients of evangelicalism are:

- Conversion, or the belief that lives need to be changed
- Biblicism, or the belief that all spiritual truth is to be found in the Bible
- Crucicentrism, or a focus on Christ's redeeming work on the cross
- Activism, or a dedication for sharing the faith and the gospel to other societies

Bebbington describes how the revivals in England in the eighteenth and early nineteenth centuries led by George Whitefield and John and Charles Wesley in turn influenced prominent figures like John Newton, Countess Selina of Huntingdon, Sir Charles and Lady Middleton, William Wilberforce, and Hannah More. Not all eighteenth or nineteenth century Evangelicals[1] would have described themselves using the above criteria, yet all would have acknowledged a type of conversion experience in their lives, although not instantaneously. All energetically sought to share widely the gospel and its reforming ideals as found in the Bible. All focused on Christ's redeeming work on the cross, and all brought new

---

1   The capitalization of "Evangelical" by most historians refers to the religious fervor exclusively among Anglicans between 1780 and 1850 in England (Bradley, the *Call to Seriousness*, 16), although Bebbington applies the capital "E" to any ardently Protestant thought. Small "e" evangelicals can refer to any adherents to the above ingredients or to a member of an evangelical church throughout the world. To avoid confusion, his book will use small "e" when referring to evangelicals in both England and the Americas.

vitality into the established churches of their day, often encountering criticism and reproach.

Evangelicalism is often widely seen as both political and religious in nature, a combination that can be distasteful to many. Modern American evangelicals may have more work to do in explaining to the rest of the world who they really are. Distinctives exist across many denominations and organizations. Yet, all are held together by their faith experiences claiming the above benchmarks. (For further reading, see Brian Harris: "Beyond Bebbington: The Quest for Evangelical Identity in a Post-modern Era," in the journal *Churchman,* 2007. www.biblicalstudies. org.uk/pdf/churchman/122-03_201.pdf.)

Mary Anne Phemister

October, 2014

Foreword

Mary Anne Phemister, when inviting me to write this introduction, sent me, among other things, a postcard-sized photo of an iconic picture of Hannah More. I doubt whether Miss More had much room in her heart and mind for icons, the proto-Victorian that she appears to have been. (Victoria did not ascend to the throne until four years after More's death.) Still, representations of More in portraits or print inspired a generation of her fellow citizens to pursue works of mercy, and she was a model for godly living. Today, one wonders whether such a portrayal would inspire young women—and young men!—of faith, goodwill, and energy to lure anyone to read up on her, to say nothing of following her.

Phemister ponders the question: Why is More so neglected, even—horrors!—forgotten today, in need of the revisiting this book provides? Why did the twentieth-century feminists who devoted themselves to Jane Austen and admired Mary Wollstonecraft not include her in their gallery of heroines for inspiration? For that matter, why don't evangelicals more readily invoke her as a celebrity? Have them list what they look for in women: they are likely to mention intelligence, courage, tenacity, exemplarity, and more, all of which she had in abundance.

Let me play the game of using a word that showed up in line three above: she may be labeled proto-Victorian, yet too few appreciate what "Victorian" connotes today. Especially most non-Austen women of that era come across as self-righteous, affectedly pious, judgmental, distant, and artless. How about Hannah More; is she well typed in such stereotype? Let us count some ways in her case. Take the "self" in "self-righteous" and you will find someone who, in contrast to the image, manifested forms of righteousness that always had "the other," not the self, in focus. Secondly, "pious"? Yes, she was pious, if we have room in the image for people whose hands are not only folded in prayer but open for helping others. Judgmental? There was much to judge, and she judged, but using biblical and classic approaches to justice. Fourth: Victorians are distant? Hardly in this case. She was a bridge-builder, someone who reached out. Finally, artless? The book's subtitle is accurate; it tells us that she was a reformer, but she was an "artist as reformer."

In sum, Hannah More is a candidate for what post- or non- or anti-Victorians who are serious and zestful about life claim to be seeking. This heroine came along at a decisive moment in British history, and she was a decider who helped others reevaluate their national, churchly, and personal lives. She was a Bluestocking when in her club, the term referred to literate, pace-setting women, challengers to those who are now uneasy with standard setters. Readers will here find chapters that show how, far from being on the margins of society, More mingled with celebrities, back when some celebrities were people of substance. Those who know anything about her era will recognize names like Newton, Walpole, and Wilberforce, people who might have drawn paparazzi to glorify themselves, but More and Company turned their mutual acquaintanceship to reformist public purposes.

Make room for Hannah More then, who, in this book's telling, was ahead of her time, but also in this book's account, did not let the bounds set by her times confine her. She outlived her family, and outlasting most critics back when life expectancy was much shorter than it is now, wrote eleven books after age sixty. Those who are still stuck with icons and stereotypes of stuffy Victorians will find unstuffy alternatives in Hannah More and her company. It is time to re-meet them, and be ready to let them change our images of them, and be changed ourselves.

—Martin E. Marty, Professor Emeritus of Church History, University of Chicago

～～～～

"Love never reasons, but profusely gives; it gives like a thoughtless prodigal its all, and then trembles least it has done too little."
Hannah More

～～～～

HANNAH MORE IS REDISCOVERED

"Caressed by princes and nobles, the delight of intellectual society, the center around which so many luminaries revolved, having her name echoed from shore to shore through the civilized world, [Hannah More] was yet a plain, home-bred, practical, and true-hearted woman."

Thus wrote her first biographer, William Roberts, in 1834 (vol. II, 434). Samuel Johnson called her "the most skilled versificatrix in the English Language." David Garrick, the great Shakespearean actor, nicknamed her "Nine," because he thought her the very personification of the nine muses. William Wilberforce sought her aid in his campaign against the slave trade. In her time, she was better known than Jane Austen or Mary Wollstonecraft. Her now-forgotten play, *Percy,* packed out Covent Garden and was the most successful tragedy of its day.

She figured in several biographical series with titles such as *Women of Worth* and *Lives of Eminent and Illustrious Englishwomen.* Then, as "Victorian values" came under attack, so did Hannah More—the epitome of those values. She became a hate object to both the radicals and conservatives who despised her evangelical sentiments. Despite being "caressed by princes and nobles," Hannah's popularity also made her the object of spiteful, narrow-minded comments from the opposite side of the spectrum. One detractor called her "the Old Bishop in Petticoats" (William

Cobbett as quoted in Mellor, 22). Another mean-spirited attacker base-lessly accused her of prostitution. Despite the cynics and naysayers, Hannah More excelled as a valuable role model for many progressive evangelical women who came later. Some commend her as a gentle mid-wife, living under the constraints of her time yet ushering in a new age for the educated woman.

In the face of all the fame she acquired during her lifetime, it is diffi-cult to believe that she would be almost completely forgotten in a hundred years. Although downgraded to the margins of our time, vestiges of her achievements remain. Her name lives on in the Hannah More School for emotionally disturbed adolescents in Baltimore, Maryland—the successor to the Hannah More Academy, founded in 1832 by an American admirer. Teachers and pupils at the Hannah More School in Nailsea, Somerset, walk by her name every day. This modern school stands near the small Sunday school Hannah founded over 230 years ago for the ragged children of min-ers and glassworkers. While visiting Bristol, one can locate the lively Han-nah More Primary School. In Wrington, a person may call on residents in the area named the Hannah More Close. In Gambier, Ohio, at Kenyon College, a candidate can apply for the Hannah More Scholarship, although few contemporary students have ever heard of her.

This pictorial biography celebrates once again Hannah More's God-gifted genius with words that helped to prevent a revolution in England as well as to give inspiration to the abolitionist movement. Hannah More's faith remained central to her life. Happily, in these pages, she has been rediscovered.

Modern literary critics find it difficult to deal with Hannah More because of her conservative evangelical perspectives. Some consider her works too moralistic and hopelessly out of vogue. They overlook the impor-tant role she played in the abolition of slavery, the education of the poor, the improvement in the manners of the great, and the morals of the many. Professor Karen Prior points out that More's only novel, *Cœlebs in Search of a Wife*, contributed to the popularization of the "religious novel" and

Hannah More (1745–1833), Martha Washington (1731–1802), Abigail Adams (1744–1818). Gilbert Stuart, artist.

The well-known portrait artist, Gilbert Stuart, famous for painting five American presidents—Washington, Adams, Jefferson, Madison, and Monroe—also painted these two extraordinary American women and a contemporary British woman named Hannah More. Stuart probably met More as a result of his association with the famed English portraitist Sir Joshua Reynolds, with whom he studied in London. Women dressed quite similarly on both sides of the Atlantic. Many, like Abigail Adams, strongly advocated for married women's property rights, and like Hannah, promoted more opportunities for women, especially in the field of education. Abigail is known for her March 1776 letter to her husband John, who was attending the Continental Congress: "Remember the Ladies . . . Do not put unlimited power in the hands of the husbands."

paved the way for the acceptability of novels within the evangelical movement of that time (Prior, 5).

What C.S. Lewis calls "chronological snobbery" may be the reason Hannah More has been overlooked. This he defined in *Surprised by Joy*, chapter 8, as "the uncritical acceptance of the intellectual climate of our own age and the assumption that whatever has gone out of date is on that account discredited." One must find out *why* something went out of date, Lewis insists. Was it true, or false? Or did it merely die away, as fashions do? Later in her life, Hannah identified herself as an evangelical. She collaborated with William Wilberforce and other evangelicals in a group that became known derisively as the Clapham Sect (or "the Clapham Saints") to champion the abolition of the slave trade and later the emancipation of all slaves held in Great Britain and her far-flung empire. The truth of the moral sin of slavery motivated this Christian group to shake the existing system.

Many books and articles clutter the shelves of feminist literary critics who continually search for early champions of women's liberation. During the past several decades, they have sifted through eighteenth- and nineteenth-century literature and writings by women, looking for evidence of latent feminism. Hannah More may not have been on the same page in promoting women's rights as Mary Wollstonecraft (1759–1797) in *A Vindication of the Rights of Women* (1792), but both writers certainly would have agreed on promoting the education of women. Hannah More, by her one novel, alone outsold Jane Austen's three novels published during Austen's lifetime, but Hannah More is little remembered today.

Born into obscurity, Hannah More died leaving nearly £30,000 (today's equivalent of almost $2,000,000)—an unimagined amount for a woman writer of two hundred years ago. The remarkable sales and popularity of her writings earned Hannah a prominent place among her contemporaries, both in social and religious circles. Due to her generous support of early missionary endeavors, we might imagine girls in Africa named after her. Moreover, her works received considerable attention in the eighteenth and nineteenth centuries among American audiences. Readers today can take courage from her strong faith and resilience in the face of adversity, and having come to know her story, perhaps may even be inclined to name a daughter Hannah.

CHAPTER 1

FISHPONDS AND BEYOND

*"It is not so important to know everything as to know
the exact value of everything, to appreciate what we learn,
and to arrange what we know."*

When little Hannah More sat by the fire learning to read and write in the company of her three older sisters, she never dreamed she would become one of the most important English women of her time. Extensive reading and writing together as a family helped to bestow on her the valuable tools Hannah's eager young mind would need in order to develop her earlier "scribblings," as she called them, to her famous mature writings. Like a deluge following a rainstorm, her writings produced an open channel for other women writers to boldly follow and successfully publish their works.

Hannah was born on February 2, 1745, in Fishponds, near Bristol, into a world of violent contrasts. As Charles Dickens expressed in his opening to *A Tale of Two Cities*, "It was the best of times, it was the worst of times." Her long life spanned the American Revolution, the French Revolution, and the Napoleonic Wars. She lived through the reigns of four British kings: George II, III, IV and William IV.

Hannah's father, Jacob More, a teacher, came from Norfolk in the North but moved to Bristol in the West Country of England after he allegedly lost a fortune in a lawsuit over land rights. Starting out a new life, he found employment as headmaster of a free school in Fishponds through his friend Lord Botetourt.

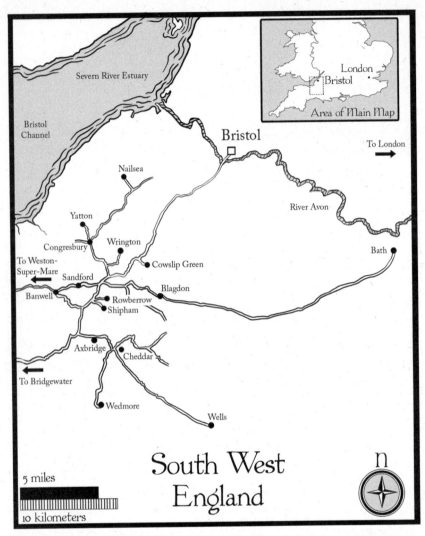

Map of England highlighting Bristol and neighboring cities of note where Hannah and her sisters opened schools. (Map by Adam Fitzgerald, used with permission.)

Hannah's birth house in Fishponds, now a neighborhood included in the larger city of Bristol. Little did young Hannah realize as she studied the classics at her father's knee in this humble stone house "in the provinces" that she would become widely known as one of the most influential female philanthropists of her day. The right side of the family home also served as a small charity school. (Photo courtesy of Bob and Anne Powell, taken May 22, 2012.)

In those days, it had become fashionable for some landowners to establish schools for the working poor, and Jacob More's landowner friend needed a good principal and teacher for his school. Jacob married Mary, the daughter of a successful farmer, who bore five bright daughters—Mary, Elizabeth, Sarah (Sally), Hannah, and Martha (Patty). Jacob happily educated all five of his daughters, but he cut short Hannah's mathematics lessons when he realized that she soaked them up so willingly. He feared that, as a girl, she would be mocked for excelling in this supposedly masculine subject. Later, she would write about the unfortunate censures placed upon female education in *Strictures on the Modern System of Female Education,* published in 1799. Mother Mary provided the practical example in the domestic arts, an important part of a girl's education. All the girls became teachers like their father; all later established their own prestigious schools; all were able to purchase property from their own earnings—outstanding achievements for women over two hundred years ago.

The more prosperous merchants of Bristol wanted their daughters educated as gentlewomen with the ability to read, write, and manage the household accounts. As the More sisters grew, their father equipped them to teach in the several private schools in the area at a time when no public schools existed. Teaching was the family business and quite unusual at that time. In most middle-class households in the eighteenth century, the "family business" often lay in finding suitable husbands for the daughters. But not in the More family. To the astonishment of many, none of Jacob and Mary's daughters married. These highly individualist sisters doubtless had their quarrels, but they achieved a harmonious, interdependent life, bound together by common goals. The girls provided for themselves through their earnings as schoolteachers and were able to retire in comfort. If they had married, their incomes, by law, would have belonged to their husbands, as well as the children the marriage would have produced.

Hannah, especially, was remarkably precocious. Before she was four, she could repeat the Anglican Catechism. Much to the amazement of her minister, she asked questions beyond her age. She studied Latin, Greek, and some mathematics under her father; later, she studied French under her older sister, Mary. At age twelve, she was composing short essays. At sixteen, she met the Scottish astronomer James Ferguson (1710–1776), from whom she gained knowledge in science. (She also helped get his papers ready for publication.[2]) Hannah's religious training began in her home and continued with Dr. James Stonhouse, a Bristol clergyman and physician who remained a lifelong friend. Later, William Wilberforce, John Wesley, John Newton, and others furthered her intense interest in how religion (and Christianity in particular) was foundational to the morals of a nation.

---

2   As quoted in Stott, 12.

Bristol, England's second commercial city of importance in the mid-eighteenth century, was a thriving town on the Severn River. Profits arose from textile and glass manufacturing, metal foundries, and especially the slave trade. It had a fine port connected to London by a good coach road. Shipping merchants loaded their ships at the Bristol docks with cloth, glass, and other items to sell to the slave traffickers in West Africa. There they would reload their ships with slaves and transport them to the West Indies and the Americas. (Image courtesy of the Bristol Port Co.)

The Clifton Suspension Bridge, spanning the picturesque Avon Gorge, is the symbol of the modern city of Bristol. Hannah More died thirty-one years before the completion of Isambard Kingdom Brunel's engineering masterpiece in 1864. During the last five years of her life, Hannah lived in the residences in the upper right of this photo, at 4 Windsor Terrace. Always a bustling port city, a new deep-sea container terminal is planned at Avonmouth in the Severn Estuary. (Photo courtesy Clifton Suspension Bridge-9350 by Gothic—own work)

In the Americas and the Caribbean islands, the slaves worked in the sugarcane, tobacco, and cotton fields. The empty ships, loaded with cotton, tobacco, sugar, and rum, returned to England. The segment of the shipping triangle between Africa and the Americas was known as the Middle Passage.

Hannah's famous work, *Slavery: a Poem* (1788), described the evils of slavery—just one of her efforts to halt slave trafficking on British ships leaving her hometown. She also joined the effort to boycott sugar if it came from slave plantations. Not until 1807 did Parliament finally pass the Abolition of the Slave Trade Act. (Courtesy of pbs.org)

CHAPTER 2

THE FAILED MARRIAGE PROPOSAL

"Goals help you overcome short-term problems."

Vivacious and attractive, Hannah starred as the charmer in her family. She exhibited "delicately refined features with beautiful keen dark eyes, enhanced [after visiting London] by the whiteness of her powdered hair," declared Henry Thompson in his early biography *The Life of Hannah More* (1838). In the eighteenth century, it was fashionable for many men to wear white wigs and for women to lightly powder their hair with a starch powder often scented with lavender and orange blossom.

Hannah's first romantic attachment was to William Turner, Esquire. Twenty years her senior, he owned a fine estate called Belmont, near Wraxhall, six miles from Bristol. Hannah met him through his cousins, who were pupils at the school where she taught. Mr. Turner found this lively schoolteacher with a pleasing personality much to his liking and proposed marriage to her. Some thought that if she married this wealthy man, she could regain for her family the security her father had lost with his failed inheritance.

After Hannah had accepted Mr. Turner's proposal, she prepared her wardrobe with things she required to be mistress of a landed estate. Besides the gowns, petticoats, shoes, and hats, she would need practical clothes for riding, travelling, and walking outdoors. While waiting for the wedding, she studied foreign languages and wrote poetry and plays for children to perform in the schools where she taught. Mr. Turner, also a poetry lover, had some of her verses carved into placards on wood and stone and placed around his estate. However, over the long, seven-year period of their engagement, Mr. Turner put off the wedding date three times. By the third postponement, Hannah had had enough. Some may say Mr. Turner was too overwhelmed and frightened by this spirited, intelligent young woman. Others think he was content to remain a bachelor. He actually begged for a fourth chance to marry Hannah, but she refused.

Upon learning of the third postponement, Hannah's friend, the Reverend Dr. James Stonhouse, from whom she had learned her catechism, reproached Mr. Turner for his conduct and the humiliation he had caused Hannah by permitting her to become the object of gossip in the community. People had begun to wonder what was wrong with Hannah. No one suggested that Mr. Turner might be the one with cold feet.

The prolonged engagement had removed Hannah from eligibility to other suitors for seven full years—all during the vibrant bloom of her youth. As compensation and to assuage his guilt, Mr. Turner agreed to give Hannah an annual payment of £200 a year for the rest of her life—about $33,000 a year at today's value. Little did Mr. Turner anticipate that Hannah would live to her eighty-ninth year! At first she refused to take the money, but later, persuaded by her sisters and Dr. Stonhouse, Hannah changed her mind and accepted it. Instead of living the life of a kept woman in a lovely estate house, she now became an independent gentlewoman, but without the restraints of managing a large household. Hannah now could turn to writing full-time.

Throughout Hannah's life, people sought her out for her brilliant wit and conversational skills. Other men proposed marriage, but she never accepted. After the breakup, Hannah is said to have resolved never to marry. Mr. Turner also never married. On at least one occasion he was invited to, and attended, one of her renowned school picnics in the Mendip Hills—an end-of-term feature attended by many of the villagers from the new schools Hannah and her sisters had set up. Hannah amiably sent him a copy of each of her books when they came out. He graciously remembered her in his will, leaving her an additional £1000 at his death.

In England and the American Colonies at that time, women could not vote and could not govern. Married women could not even own property. In the case of divorce, women could not keep their children; children were considered the property of the husband. Before the Married Woman's Property Act, passed in England in 1870, married women had few legal rights. By contrast, single and widowed women were considered a separate legal being—a *feme sole*—and could own property in their own names. Hannah More's decision not to marry thus enabled her to keep her income from her writings and give it away to worthy projects

The Belmont Estate, Wraxall, North Somerset. It has recently undergone extensive renovation by its current owner. Formerly part of the Tyntesfield Estate, Belmont House is now a private residence with views looking down on the Bristol Channel. When this book went to press, the Belmont Estate was for sale at over $5 million. The National Trust bought the separated Tyntesfield Estate property in 2002, following the death of the owner, Lord Wraxall, in 2001. After refurbishment, Tyntesfield and its gardens are open to visitors.

as she pleased, which she did with great generosity. Hannah still could not vote nor be elected to Parliament. Those privileges were not granted to women until 1918, and then only to those women over the age of thirty who met the minimum property qualifications. Ten years later, however, in 1928, Parliament extended voting rights to all women over the age of twenty-one, and on the same terms as men.

Hannah More, c. 1780, by Frances Reynolds, sister of the renowned painter Sir Joshua Reynolds. This portrait portrays the poet in a gentle, pensive mood, but without powdered hair, a fashion of the day. She is simply but elegantly dressed with a discreet suggestion of pearls in her hair. She is shown writing a letter with a quill pen reflectively facing the viewer. Reproduced with kind permission from the Bridgeman Art Library.

An area known as "The Rocks" stretches along the southern slopes near Belmont House. Various quarries in the area served as rich sources of building material. The red sandstone strata, when left exposed, appeared to bleed, especially after rain. Hannah wrote her poem "The Bleeding Rock" (1773) about a rejected lover who turned to stone (except for his heart, which bled when struck). The "weeping" rock strata in the Wraxall area provided the visual metaphor for the sadness she must have felt after Mr. Turner kept postponing their wedding date.

> *The guiltless steel assailed the mortal part*
> *And stabbed the vital, vulnerable heart.*
> *The life-blood issuing from the wounded stone,*
> *Blends with the crimson current of his own.*
> (Excerpt from "The Bleeding Rock" by Hannah More)*[3]*

---

3 For further information re rock strata in Somerset see article by Robert J. Evered in *Bristol and Avon Family History Society Journal,* June 2002, and posted on their website under "Wraxall.")

CHAPTER 3

HANNAH'S FIRST PLAYS AND EARLY FRIENDSHIP WITH THE GREAT DAVID GARRICK

"We are apt to mistake our vocation in looking out of the way for occasions to exercise great and rare virtues, and step over the ordinary ones which lie directly in the road before us."

A t an early age, Hannah found that the young people in her circle liked putting on plays, but many plays circulating in those days lacked high moral content. So at age seventeen, she wrote *The Search for Happiness,* a little drama for the girls at the school where she was teaching. In the play, four female characters groan about their woes and sad lives. They come upon a wise shepherdess who counsels the girls to quit singing their laments and to get an education while at the same time cultivating domestic virtues—the art of running a household. She cautioned them to be wary of seeking fame and fortune. Ten years later, this simple play found a publisher in London and proceeded on to twelve editions, finding regular performances in girls' schools across the country. Little did Hannah know that her writings as a teenager, based on her own nontraditional but excellent education, would bring her fame and fortune.

While Hannah awaited her wealthy fiancé's decision on a wedding date, she studied, and proved especially gifted in Latin, Italian, French, and Spanish. To further cultivate her mind and her literary pursuits, she used her time to read and translate celebrated authors. Still living in

Publisher Thomas Cadell (1742–1802) had offices in both Bristol and London. He had the good fortune of taking on this relatively unknown poet and began publishing most of Hannah's works—both prose and poetry. In her early days, she knew little about publishers; she sold him the copyright to *The Search for Happiness,* first published in Bristol by Sarah Farley in 1773. By 1800, she had sold over ten thousand copies. Later, as Hannah became a hot literary property, she learned to drive a better bargain. Thomas Cadell also published works by noted literary giant Samuel Johnson, the novelist Fanny Burney, and the poet Robert Burns, among other notables.

Bristol, Hannah often attended the theater, first the Jacob's Well Theatre and later the New Theatre at King's Street. She became acquainted with several well-known actors of the day and longed to have one of her plays featured in an important theater. Attending the theater was a popular entertainment for many people in the eighteenth century, two hundred years before television.

Eager to provide more suitable material for her pupils to perform in school, Hannah wrote other short dramas based on Old Testament stories. These appeared as *Sacred Dramas* (1782). Now twenty-eight and exasperated at being trifled with by her erstwhile suitor, she could at last set her sails to visit London—a long-cherished wish—and find a publisher.

The Reverend Dr. James Stonhouse, who had secured the annuity of £200 a year after the seven-year engagement debacle with Mr. William Turner, Esq., now performed another great service for Hannah. He sent a manuscript copy of one of her plays, *The Inflexible Captive,* with a cover letter, to his friend David Garrick.

The greatest Shakespearian actor of his day, David Garrick (1717–1779) had become a man of great influence in London. The possible contact with

David and Eva Marie Garrick. Garrick, the lead-ing actor-manager of the 1700s, revolutionized English theater with a lively, naturalistic acting style that held audiences spellbound. Indeed, he shone as one of the most astonishing Brit-ish personalities in a time when the country was brimming with astonishing personalities. (Photo courtesy of the Folger Library, Washington, DC, which holds thousands of manuscripts, including verses, plays, letters, Drury Lane accounts, clip-pings, periodicals, prints, paintings, books, and other materials and artifacts that span Garrick's personal and professional life.)

the legendary Mr. Garrick certainly prompted Hannah's visit to London, the first of at least thirty-five visits she would make. Two of her sisters, Sarah (Sally) and Martha (Patty), accompanied her on this first visit in 1773, but she did not meet her soon-to-be idol at that time. A good deal of her time she spent sick in bed with a fever. Garrick himself was ill and not performing. Frustrated, the party of three returned to Bristol. This first venture into a bleak, wintry London ended up a dismal, expensive failure.

However, within days of her second arrival in London by stagecoach in 1774, Hannah was introduced to David Garrick and his wife, Eva Marie. During this visit, Hannah met Elizabeth Montagu, who would become a lifelong friend. She also met the artist Sir Joshua Reynolds, who in turn introduced her to Dr. Samuel Johnson—now famous for his massive *Dictionary of the English Language*—and Johnson's friend James Boswell, who often travelled with Johnson. Boswell would later write the brilliant biography *The Life of Samuel Johnson*.

Both Johnson and Boswell were instantly charmed by the witty young lady from Bristol and sought her company when they attended society functions. Boswell would tease her by calling her "Holy Han-nah"; nevertheless, he had enormous respect for her religious principles and her writings. Samuel Johnson, on the other hand, felt a kindred spirit with Hannah and her spiritual values. She quickly forged enduring friendships with Edmund Burke, Elizabeth Carter, Sir Joshua Reynolds, and his sister Frances Reynolds. Miss Reynolds, also an artist, would later paint Hannah's portrait.

Although Mr. Garrick did not stage *The Inflexible Captive* at the Drury Lane Theatre as Hannah had hoped, he opened his social circle to her. She would wait two years before her play was performed on stage at the Theatre Royal in the town of Bath. Meanwhile, a deep friendship developed with David Garrick and his wife Eva Marie. David nicknamed

The Theatre Royal in Bath, over two hundred years old, is one of the more important theatres in the United Kingdom outside London. Refurbished in 2010 at a cost of £3 million (about $5 million), the nine-hundred-seat theater hosts many plays before their official opening in London. Hannah's plays were often performed there. (Photo courtesy of the Theatre Royal.)

Edmund Burke (1729–1797). Born in Ireland to a Protestant father, he moved to Bristol, where he represented the Bristol area in Parliament. He is remembered mainly for his support of the cause of the American revolutionaries and for his later opposition to the French Revolution. Some view him as the philosophical founder of modern conservatism. He is famous for saying: "The only thing necessary for the triumph of evil is for good men to do nothing" and "Those who do not learn from history are destined to repeat it."

her "Nine" because he said Hannah embodied all the nine muses. He noted her talent and carefully nurtured and championed her work among his broad circle of friends and acquaintances. Nothing could have been of greater encouragement to a young, blossoming female playwright of the time.

In 1777, David Garrick helped Hannah achieve her great triumph on the London stage. She was only thirty-two. To show his confidence in Hannah's work, he acted in her new play, *Percy,* the sad and dramatic tale of feuding families in England and Scotland. It had a run of nineteen performances to enthusiastic audiences at the Covent Garden Theatre. Mr. Garrick's support, followed by good reviews, rocketed Hannah like a shooting star onto the London scene.

Garrick beamed with pride over his new protégée. However, Hannah seemed a bit conflicted about her new celebrity. Fame had its drawbacks. Although most of the reviews sounded favorable, Hannah learned of some spiteful comments directed at her from others in London society. She became physically ill, which was often the way her body responded to the stress of unkind criticism throughout her life. At that time, women were not empowered to speak out forcefully in their own defense. Often, the emotional pain unconsciously transformed itself into actual physical discomfort, a phenomenon still common today and a type of PTSD (post-traumatic stress disorder).

In the spring, after her Covent Garden triumph, she returned to her hometown, where *Percy* was performed, again for a full house. Much encouraged, Hannah set about writing a third play, *The Fatal Falsehood* (1779), which she completed after Garrick's death. Without Garrick's substantial support, the play was not as successful. She never wrote for the London stage again.

During Hannah's visits to London, her friendship with Mr. and Mrs. Garrick deepened. She often was invited to stay with the Garricks at their townhouse in London and at their villa, Hampton, on the banks of the River Thames. She was like a daughter to this childless couple. Hannah frequently accompanied them on their visits to their celebrity friends, who found her enchanting and delightful. She made friends wherever she went. Hannah admired David Garrick immensely, and her feelings for him ran strong and deep, but there is not the slightest suggestion that her affections for him were other than platonic. He was like a father figure to her, in much the same way as her lifelong male friends Bishop Porteus, Horace Walpole, Samuel Johnson, John Newton, and William Wilberforce became part of her ever-enlarging circle. Men always seemed attracted to her for her clever wit, astute observations, and lively conversational skills.

At that time, London had about five hundred thousand inhabitants, no sewer system, only primitive street lighting, and many slums. Garbage was thrown into the River Thames, which served as the main water supply of the city as well as the great river road to the North Sea. Named and

The Garricks' villa, Hampton, on the banks of the Thames River, with a monument to Shakespeare on the left. Hannah More spent much time at Hampton from 1776, and after David Garrick's death in 1779, she spent twenty winters as companion to his widow, Eva Marie.

Fire broke out on the roof of Hampton House, October 25, 2008, while a workman with a blowtorch was working near the top of the wooden pillars in a gale. This disastrous fire followed others at Windsor Castle (1992) and Hampton Court (1986) and raised serious questions about the use of blow-torches, candles, and other potentially dangerous incendiary devices in historic buildings. (Photograph used by the kindness of John Inglis, ARPS)

unnamed infectious diseases proliferated. Horse-drawn vehicles pro-vided the only means of transportation inland, unless a person walked or rode a horse. It is necessary to bear in mind the huge gap between the wealthy and the poor at that time. Even "polite society," those who could afford carriages, flaunted shocking profanity, coarse jokes, and vulgar words symptomatic of moral decay. Religion for most had become the object of jest, indifference, or skeptical hostility. Although the English Bible was in the people's hands, it was almost a dead book, seldom read. Despite her deep friendships and influential connections, Hannah had to be very careful of the many complex influences surrounding her in all levels of society in the "vanity fair" of London.

Despite a growing antagonism to religion and ignorance of the Christian gospel, the voice of awakening began to whisper throughout the land like leaves fluttering in a warm summer breeze. A few brave Church of England ministers, most notably George Whitfield (1717–1770) and John Wesley (1703–1791), preached in the open air to great crowds, individuals who might never enter the door of a church because they lacked appropriate dress. These clergymen also prayed extemporaneously, not limiting themselves to written prayers. The Book of Common Prayer (1662) was still part of their heritage, but they did not bind themselves to it or to the prescribed sermons the bishops distributed for Sunday homilies. Their sermons often came from Bible texts, calling their listeners to repent of their sins and begin a new life of holiness to God. Intense revivalism began to reach the harsher landscapes and byways of England. The established Church of England looked upon the growing numbers of itinerant preachers as fanatical spreaders of radical religionist teaching, similar to the Puritan dissenters. "Methodism" ranked dangerously close to apostasy in the minds of many. Nevertheless, this wave of religious rejuvenation slowly began to touch the highest circles of London society. Hannah would soon find her own faith revitalized.

David Garrick died in London on January 20, 1779, just a few weeks shy of his sixty-second birthday. He was by all accounts a faithful and devoted husband to Eva Marie Veigel, a charming Viennese dancer whom he married in 1749. He claimed that after their marriage, he never passed a night

George Whitefield (1717–1770) traveled seven times to the American Colonies, becoming good friends with Benjamin Franklin, who helped to support Whitefield's orphanage in Georgia. John and Charles Wesley followed some of Whitefield's practices, such as preaching out of doors to people marginalized by the established church.

Countess Lady Selina Huntingdon (1707–1791) and the chapel she helped build in Bath. The restored chapel now serves as the town's information center.

Sarah Crosby (1729–1804) and Lady Selina Huntingdon are examples of women who journeyed up and down the country proclaiming the good tidings of God's salvation. They preached and held prayer and Bible study meetings but were not ordained.

(Photos courtesy of Wikipedia.)

away from her. She survived her husband by forty-three years, living quietly, mainly at their estate in Hampton, and devoting herself to perpetuating his memory. She died on October 16, 1822, at the age of ninety-eight, and was buried beside her "Davy" in the Poet's Corner of Westminster Abbey.

Garrick's funeral was one of the grandest ever seen in London, with the carriages of mourners stretching all the way from Westminster Abbey back to The Strand. He was buried near the monument to William Shakespeare. Samuel Johnson mourned that the great man's death had "eclipsed the gaiety of nations." Hannah More would later become a spiritual companion to her now close friend Samuel Johnson as his own death approached.

CHAPTER 4

THE BLUESTOCKING LITERARY SOCIETY

*"When you are disposed to be vain of your mental acquire-
ment, look up to those who are more accomplished than
yourself, that you may be fired with emulation; but when you
feel dissatisfied with your circumstances, look down on those
beneath you, that you may learn contentment."*

Some historians have divided Hannah's life into four periods. During the first period she was a teacher; during the second, a writer of
plays and poetry; in the third, a member of the famous "Bluestocking Literary Society" in London; and during the fourth, a social reformer
and philanthropist. Others have simply partitioned her life into two periods: before and after her conversion to evangelical Christianity. Hannah
always considered herself a Christian, always remained a member of the
Church of England, always continued her active life with her Bluestocking friends, but after reading Puritan and dissenting authors,[4] Hannah
became more committed to following Christ attentively.

Who were the Bluestockings and how did they get their name? The
English term *Bluestocking* refers to a group of literary women in society

---

4   Those who separated themselves from the established or national church.
    In England this term covered Presbyterians, Congregationalists, Baptists,
    Methodists, and Roman Catholics from 1662 to c. 1850. About midcentury,
    nonconformist replaced the term *dissenter*.

Elizabeth Montagu, the "Queen of the Blues," by Thomas Cheesman, after a portrait by Sir Joshua Reynolds. Hannah praised Mrs. Montagu for her "27 years of uninterrupted warmth and kindness."

who were beginning to express their boredom with being sent off to play cards or do their embroidery rather than engaging in after-dinner conversation with the men. Often women were left at home while husbands attended their "clubs" or their men-only society meetings.

Around 1750, the Shakespeare scholar Mrs. Elizabeth Montagu, later known as the "queen of the Bluestockings," founded the first Bluestocking Society in London. These learned ladies, unlike the exclusive men's clubs, often invited members of the opposite sex to join them to talk about books, literature, art, architecture, education, and the many events that interested them. Other women who attended these gatherings were Elizabeth Carter (1717–1806), who translated *Epictetus* from the Greek; Fanny Burney (1752–1840), a novelist; Elizabeth Vesey (1715–91), the vivacious hostess; Catharine Macaulay (1739–91), an historian; and Frances Boscawen (1719–1805), hostess, letter writer, and widow of a famous British admiral.

Scholars dispute the origins of the name. Some say European fashion in the mid-eighteenth century dictated that white stockings be worn for formal wear and blue stockings for daytime and more informal wear.[5] Many historians claim that the term derived from the first visit of the learned botanist and publisher Benjamin Stillingfleet. The story claims that Mr. Stillingfleet was not rich enough to robe his legs in white silk

---

5   Anne Buck, *Dress in Eighteenth-Century England* (New York: Holmes and Meier, 1979), 138.

Benjamin Stillingfleet, botanist (1702–1771), an early male attender of the ladies' Bluestocking Literary Society.

stockings, so Mrs. Vesey, one of the group's founders, simply advised him to "come in your blue stockings." The term came to refer to the informal quality of the gatherings that placed emphasis on enlightened conversation over fashion. More widely, the phrase *Bluestocking* came to refer to any learned or intellectual women—in French, *bas-bleu*. Periodicals and newspapers picked up the term to describe this fairly new phenomenon of women who wrote, published, and pursued the life of the mind.

Mrs. Montagu invited Hannah to join this group whenever she visited London. To show her appreciation, Hannah wrote "The Bas Blue," a lighthearted poem that amused her new group of friends. Even Samuel Johnson, who had a reputation for harsh criticism, was particularly entertained by the poem. Dr. Johnson, famous for his *Dictionary,* essays, and *Lives of the Poets,* had his own literary circle, but the ladies were not invited. Both Johnson and More were considered "the moralists" due to their high view of Christian ethics.

Samuel Johnson starred as a pivotal figure among the Bluestockings. They all read his *Rambler* essays, admired his *Dictionary,* and knew of his influence as a literary critic. He seemed highly susceptible to female

The Nine Living Muses of Great Britain, 1779, by Richard Samuel. More is Melpomene, the Muse of Tragedy, the figure holding the cup. Others are Elizabeth Carter, the classics scholar; Angelica Kauffmann, the portraitist; Anna Laetitia Barbauld, the poet; Catharine Macaulay, the historian; Elizabeth Montagu, the patron of the arts and literary critic; Elizabeth Griffith, the actress and playwright; Elizabeth Ann Sheridan, the singer; and Charlotte Lennox, the novelist. (Picture courtesy of the National Portrait Gallery, London.)

charm and more appreciative of the female mind than many of his contemporaries. Some historians think Mrs. Montagu invited the young Mrs. Hester Thrale, the wealthy brewer's wife, into the group because of Hester's close friendship with Mr. Johnson. During one of Johnson's deep periods of depression, Mrs. Thrale had invited him to spend time at her home in Streatham to aid him in his recovery. As a result, Johnson often returned to the Thrale home, yet another literary salon, for the sumptuous meals her wealthy husband could provide and the conversations around the table.

In the late fall of 1778, while Hannah worked on her play *The Fatal Falsehood,* she received word that her good friend David Garrick had fallen ill. She quickly wrote to his doctor to see if she could be of any help to Eva Marie. The doctor urged her to come immediately. Hannah did so and greatly comforted Mrs. Garrick, who invited Hannah to stay with her for some time after the funeral. She became Mrs. Garrick's

Samuel Johnson (1709–1784). Biographer Peter Martin writes, "He treated women as intellectual equals and promoted their literary careers . . . His tireless charity and Christian benevolence towards the underprivileged, oppressed, and poor were well known in his lifetime." According to Sally, Hannah's sister who often accompanied her to London, Hannah was a particular favorite of  Dr. Johnson. He even memorized her poem *Sir Eldred,* reciting the lines to greet her on one occasion. Together they formed a sort of mutual admiration society.

companion, staying with her both at her London home (the Adelphi) and at her summer home (Hampton) in Middlesex. Hannah would return home to Bristol for six months and then, at Eva Marie's request, spend January to June with her.

During those months in London, Hannah often accepted invitations to dinners and the theater. She also finished *The Fatal Falsehood,* but David Garrick was no longer around to edit some of her lines and champion her cause. The play was produced at Covent Garden May 6, 1779, but to Hannah it seemed a dismal failure, running only three nights. This disappointment, coupled with the death of her mentor and several other things about which we shall later learn, led her to give up writing for the stage.

In her scholarly biography of Hannah More, Anne Stott adds an interesting postscript to More's short career as a playwright: "In 1779, the play *Percy* was translated into German, performed in Vienna, and well received. Someone found a copy of the play among Mozart's possessions after he died in 1791." Given the right librettist, Stott wonders, who knows what Mozart (1756—1791) would have done with it if he had not died at an early age (Stott, 47).

Public concerts in the second half of the eighteenth century reflected the quickened pace of the social and cultural life in London. In 1785, for example, many performances of the ever-popular *Messiah* packed out halls to celebrate the one hundredth anniversary of the birth of George Frederic Handel (1685–1759). Subscription concerts that premiered symphonies of J.S. Bach (1685–1750) and Franz Joseph Haydn (1732–1809) were conspicuous symbols of luxury.[6] We can imagine Hannah and her friends attending one of the Friday-evening private concerts hosted by Elizabeth Montagu or the very popular oratorios of Handel. Hannah preferred oratorios to the opera, because most contained biblical themes. (*Deborah, Esther, Israel in Egypt, Saul, Susanna,* and *Solomon* are among the twenty-five oratorios that Handel composed.)

The diarist and novelist Fanny Burney, another one of the younger Bluestocking women, circulated in both literary and musical circles. She achieved notice for her novels, *Evelina, Camilla,* and *Cecilia,* books that explored the lives of English aristocrats. Hannah More found Burney's novels entertaining, thought-provoking, and lively, but lacking in religion.

On one occasion, Mrs. Garrick assembled a dinner party at her home to which she invited Fanny Burney and her musicologist father, along with writer and parliamentarian Edmund Burke, Elizabeth Carter, Dr. Samuel Johnson, Hannah More, and others. Johnson later reported to his friend Boswell his great praise of Hannah, Fanny, and Eva Marie, calling them "three incomparable women." Johnson and More were known as mutual flatterers and much enjoyed each other's company on these occasions. Their mutual admiration became one of the jokes of the older women. Johnson was forty years older than Hannah. One spring, Johnson and Boswell even took the trouble to travel the bumpy coach road from London to visit Hannah and her school in Bristol.

During the last year of his life, Hannah often visited her dear old friend at his London home at 8 Bolt Court.[7] Johnson biographer Peter Martin

---

6   For more on London musical culture at this time, see Simon McVeigh, Concert Life in London from Mozart to Haydn, Cambridge University Press, 1995.

7   Earlier, while compiling his famous dictionary, Johnson lived at 17 Gough

Fanny Burney (1752–1840) is best known for her four novels, twenty volumes of diaries, and letters. Her early novels were read and enjoyed by Jane Austen, whose own *Pride and Prejudice* derives from the final pages from *Cecilia.* Her father, Charles Burney, the noted composer and musicologist, authored the multivolume *A General History of Music.* He credited the London music scene as the great preserver of the old masters.

reports, "In addition to her exemplary and modest moral nature, Hannah More provided him with the uncluttered female grace and wit he craved to keep up his spirits" (Martin, 460). After Johnson's death, she treasured the memory of having attended church with him when he took his last communion. Hannah and Johnson's bond demonstrates the truth that lasting friendships are often cemented around books, religious convictions, and conversations stimulated by reading common texts.

CHAPTER 5

IMPORTANT CALLERS AT COWSLIP GREEN

"If faith produces no works, I see faith is not a living tree. Thus faith and works together grow . . . they are soul and body, hand and heart. What God hath joined, let no man part."

Hannah More relished the social whirl of London and the attention she received from her enlarging circle of friends, but only up to a point. As noted in chapter 4, the relentless rounds at parties and plays in the big city began to wear on her. Perhaps it was the death of her father in 1783, quickly followed by the passing of Samuel Johnson in 1784, that prompted Hannah to turn toward a calmer life in the countryside. She had barely gotten over the death of her mentor David Garrick. A rural landscape seemed as good an antidote as any to remedy Hannah's discomfort. During her visits to her hometown of Bristol about every six months, she would often ride into the Mendip Hills for solitude and reflection.

Not much is known about what happened to Hannah's parents, but we do know that the daughters provided lodging for them in Bristol until both departed this life. At the time of her father's death, Hannah was staying in London with Mrs. Garrick and could not attend his burial. Roads in winter made it troublesome to travel at that time of year. (Railways did not become a popular means of transportation until the early nineteenth century, when they began to serve the needs of the burgeoning Industrial Revolution.)

Whatever her motivation, Hannah bought property twelve miles from Bristol, near the market town of Wrington. She then set about to build the country house she named Cowslip Green. Aided by her sisters, Hannah took great delight in the design and planting of the gardens. Her little thatch-roofed cottage, placed next to a farm in the West Country, became her getaway from the bustle of London. Her London friends became intrigued. Mrs. Montagu sent a couple of chairs to help with the furnishings. Horace Walpole sent books for her library from his Strawberry Press publications.

In a letter to Eva Marie Garrick, June 26, 1786, Hannah described her county retreat as "this little wild spot, where I know no more of the world or its ways than if I were in an Hermitage." (Etching courtesy of the Folger Shakespeare Library collection)

Cowslip Green, delightful as it was, bordered a pig farm. Some days, the smell kept the ladies from taking tea in the garden. This photo, taken in 2012, shows the proximity of the farm to the cottage. (Photo courtesy of William Phemister.)

Horace Walpole, son of the great prime minister, had met Hannah in London in 1780, when he was sixty-three years old and suffering with gout; she was forty at the time. Walpole never married but enjoyed flirting with the ladies, especially "safe" ones like Hannah, with whom

Horace Walpole (1717–97) by Sir Joshua Reynolds. Notice his gothic-style castle in background. Walpole published Hannah's *Florio, A Tale for Fine Gentlemen and Fine Ladies*, a long poem extolling the virtues of country life, which she dedicated to him. It was as if the lines Hannah had written about Florio's escapades had shaped her own yearning for a quieter, more pastoral setting.

> *A thousand cheerful thoughts arise,*
> *Each rural scene enchants his eyes;*
> *With transport he begins to look*
> *On Nature's all-instructive book.*

Besides being a writer in his own right (the gothic novel *The Castle of Otranto* is perhaps his best-known work), Walpole, an inveterate letter writer, would later inherit the title of Lord Orford from his father.

marriage was never a possibility. (Another of her aging male admirers was ninety-year-old General George Oglethorpe, the founder of Georgia in the American Colonies.)

Horace Walpole enjoyed Hannah's spirited company, often inviting her and Mrs. Garrick to visit him at Strawberry Hill, his gothic villa in Twicken-ham, known for its art, ceramic collections, and beautiful gardens. He loved receiving Hannah's clever letters in return to his. (Volumes of his letters are

The gallery at Strawberry Hill, 1842.

archived at the Yale University Library.) Walpole called her "Saint Hannah." Although he mocked her religious devo-tion, even in her company, he always maintained high respect for her character and writings. As he approached death, he, like Samuel John-son, sought out her comfort-ing friendship.

While Hannah oversaw the building of her own new small house in the country, she made the acquaintance in Bristol of the milkwoman Ann Yearsley (1752–1806). This friendship began warmly but soon ended bit-terly. Ann Yearsley was self-educated through books given to her mother by her mother's employers. She married a yeoman farmer and bore six children, but due to her husband's drinking, the family appeared almost destitute on the day she stopped by Hannah More's house to pick up swill for their pigs. Hannah became aware of Yearsley's poems, thought Ann talented, and arranged for the publication of some of them. With the patronage of Hannah and her Bluestocking circle, Ann Yearsley became an immediate success. However, her new fame and fortune (around £380 for her first book of poems) became the cause of their split.

Due to a concern that Ann's unstable husband would squander the Yearsley finances, Hannah, along with Elizabeth Montagu, set up

Horace Walpole's newly renovated white, gothic castle, now part of Twickenham, a western suburb of London (2010). Gothic revival architecture,
with its many turrets and shaped windows, was coming back into vogue in
the eighteenth century. (Image courtesy of Strawberry Hill House.)

a trust fund to invest Ann's income in government stocks. Before long,
Ann, under pressure from her husband, demanded the deed to the
trust so she could spend the money as she willed. She publicly accused
Hannah of high-handedness and arrogance. Ann felt she knew better
than Hannah how to handle her own affairs. Hannah's friends, however, rallied around her and accused Yearsley of shocking ingratitude.
After all, it was Hannah who had brought her poems to light and cata-
pulted her to fame.

The misfired friendship proved to be a humbling experience for Hannah, who later stated that she owed a debt to Yearsley for this cautionary
blow to her own love of fame. Perhaps this distressing business contributed

Ann Yearsley was one of only a few working-class women of the era to gain prominence as a writer. She produced poems on various subjects and in 1788 wrote "A Poem on the Inhumanity of the Slave Trade," criticizing Bristol's shipping role, a poem against slavery that Hannah certainly would appreciate. (Image courtesy of the Poetry Foundation.)

to Hannah's wish to turn away from the applause of fashionable society and seriously seek peace within her own soul.

Around this time, Hannah also made the acquaintance in London of several prominent men who would deeply influence her life—the Reverend John Newton (1725–1807), William Wilberforce (1759–1833), and the Reverend John Wesley (1703–91). A verse of one of Newton's hymns seemed to resonate with Hannah's increasingly spiritual sentiments at that time:

Savior, if of Zion's city
I through grace a member am;
Let the world deride or pity,
I will glory in thy name:
Fading is the world's best pleasures,
All its boasted pomp and show;
Solid joys and lasting treasure,
None but Zion's children know.
(*Glorious Things of Thee are Spoken*, John Newton, 1779.)

John Newton (1715–1807), former slave ship captain and author of the hymn "Amazing Grace." Newton was spiritual mentor to both Hannah More and William Wilberforce. Many of his poems found their way into the *Olney Hymnbook,* published in 1779. He visited Hannah and her sisters at Cowslip Green during the busy and demanding time when they were setting up their schools. The sisters often had to ride sidesaddle into the remote villages of the Mendip Hills, even in inclement weather. Carriages would often get stuck in the mud. Newton wondered if the ordeals of the sisters' labors were disturbing their health and cautioned them to take care. Hannah, in particular, often succumbed to various maladies, retreating to her home in Bath to spend the winters. Yet, in spite of the many periods of poor health, the resilient Hannah would outlive all of her sisters and most of her friends.

Not all was tranquil and serene for Hannah More at Cowslip Green. As noted in an earlier chapter, Hannah often became afflicted with headaches and other ailments, many brought on by the harsh criticisms she faced in the public arena, not to mention the foul winter weather. Especially troubling was the time in London after *Percy* was produced when she was falsely charged with plagiarism. Hannah simply reacted to the emotional pain she experienced in the manner socially acceptable for women in her day: she internalized in her body the distress of being unfairly accused. Hoping for respite, she would often travel to Bath to find relief in the warm, healing waters in that city.

It was in Bath in 1786 that Hannah first met William Wilberforce. He had also come to take the warm mineral waters for his many physical infirmities. Wilberforce would become her stalwart, lifelong friend. They worked together in the cause for the abolition of slavery in Great Britain, and he helped her in soliciting subscriptions for the *Cheap Repository Tracts* she would later write. Hannah and her sisters eventually bought a

The Roman baths, Somerset, UK. Since before Roman times, Bath's mineral springs have provided a tonic for those suffering from a variety of
diseases. After Queen Anne (1665–1714) frequented the baths in the early
eighteenth century, people from all over England flocked to the healing
waters, not only to drink but also to bathe in the warm springs bubbling up
from below. By 2000, Bath's hydrotherapy clinics had closed, but tourists
still flock to this world UNESCO site to visit the many structures still stand-
ing. (Image courtesy of Bath Preservation Trust.)

---

house at 76 Pulteney Street, Bath, where they would retreat in the winter
when Cowslip Green, built on a low site, became too cold and damp.

In August 1789, Wilberforce visited Cowslip Green with his sister,
the first of many visits to his dynamic new friend and her sisters. This
informal social call held special significance because it led Hannah to

the opening of schools and Sunday schools throughout Somerset and the Mendip Hills. Their pioneering mission of educating the rural poor would require thirty-two years of diligent effort but is thought by many to be the greatest and most distinctive work of Hannah's life.

Martha More, known to her family as Patty, was the youngest of the five sisters and the closest to Hannah. She wrote in her journal (later published as *The Mendip Annals* in 1859), about the incident the evening Wilberforce came to visit the famous Cheddar Gorge:

> I was in the parlour when he returned. I enquired how he liked the cliffs. He replied that they were very fine, but the poverty and distress of the people was dreadful . . . He retired to his room . . . I felt he was not well. The cold chicken and wine put into the carriage for his dinner were returned untouched. [At the evening meal] he began, "Miss Hannah More, something must be done for Cheddar."
>
> He then proceeded to a particular account of his day—of all the inquiries he had made respecting the poor. There was no resident minister, no manufactory, nor did there appear any dawn of comfort, either physical or spiritual. The method or possibility of assisting them was discussed until a late hour. It was at length decided in a few words by Mr. W's exclaiming, "If *you* will be at the trouble, *I* will be at the expense."

How much money Wilberforce gave to build Hannah More's schools will never be known, but he was instrumental in introducing her to the wealthy members of the Clapham Sect, who shared similar goals for the education of the poor. To underline his concern for and interest in these charity schools, in 1797 Wilberforce brought his young wife, Barbara Anne Spooner, on their honeymoon to show her the many schools and the friendly societies for women he and the More sisters had helped to set up. Their visit served to greatly encourage the two sisters.

William Wilberforce (1759–1833): a widely reproduced 1810 portrait of Wilberforce, age fifty-one, three years after the abolition of the slave trade. A native of Kingston on Hull, he became a Member of Parliament at twenty-three. In 1785, he underwent a conversion experience and became an evangelical Christian. This resulted in major lifestyle changes and a lifelong commitment for reform. For twenty-six years, he headed the parliamentary campaign against the British slave trade until the passage of the Slave Trade Act in 1807. This Act is not to be confused with the Slave Abolition Act, which emancipated all slaves living in England and her colonies in 1833. He also championed causes such as the Society for the Suppression of Vice, missionary work in India, the foundation of the Church Mission Society, and the Society for the Prevention of Cruelty to Animals. Wilberforce died at age seventy-four, just three days after learning that the Slave Abolition Act of 1833 had passed Parliament.

The Reverend John Newton, visiting a few years later and now in his upper sixties, also came to call on Hannah at Cowslip Green. A lonely old man with fading eyesight, Newton wrote that he had been dreaming of visiting her and her sisters and wished to enjoy their garden. The visit occurred some time after the death of Newton's wife in 1790. Some of his letters suggest that his heart may have been turning toward Hannah, but Mrs. More, as she was now respectfully known, was not planning to marry anyone. Newton was also twenty years her senior. Busy with her schools and writings, she could not even entertain the thought of caring for an old man in a romantic way.

Earlier, Newton had been skeptical of her writing plays, even her *Sacred Dramas,* due to his Puritan-induced tendency to reject going to the theater or reading imaginative literature in general. Yet Hannah, he

Hannah More's house, 76 Great Pulteney Street, Bath, England, where Hannah More lived from 1792–1802. Her first play, *The Inflexible Captive,* was staged in Bath in 1775. It was here that she wrote *Village Politics* and *Remarks on the Speech of M. DuPont*. In 1799, she published *Strictures on the Modern System of Female Education*, and she wrote and edited the *Cheap Repository Tracts*. (Images courtesy of Bath Heritage Plaques.)

now felt sure, could serve God by offering morally suitable plays to coun-
teract the less principled fare currently available for schoolchildren. She
helped to change the mind of this transformed former slave ship captain
who had also served as her spiritual mentor.

CHAPTER 6

THE CHALLENGE OF CHEDDAR AND THE MENDIP HILLS

A Mission Destined For Conflict

*"My object is not to make fanatics, but to train up the lower
classes in habits of industry and piety. I know of no way of
teaching morals but by teaching principles; nor of inculcating
Christian principles without a good knowledge of Scripture."*

After William Wilberforce's visit to the vicinity of the Cheddar Gorge, Hannah bubbled with ideas about how to set up a school in Cheddar and perhaps other schools in the neighboring villages. His now-famous challenge, "If you will be at the trouble I will be at the expense," kept ringing in her ears. Wilberforce had found the destitute inhabitants he encountered "wretchedly poor and deficient in spiritual help." Something needed to be done, and he saw hope in the skills of Hannah and her sisters.

Starting schools among the poor in the countryside east of Bristol was a mission destined to face much opposition. One civic leader even begged her not to think of bringing schools and religion into his district. He complained that education only made the poor lazy and useless. Hannah answered the suspicious, comparatively wealthy land-owning farmers with the claim that schools would be to their benefit. Schools would teach manners and morality, useful in preventing the poor from robbing

Cheddar Gorge. "Providence directed Mr. Wilberforce and his sister to spend a few days at Cowslip Green. The cliffs of Cheddar were esteemed a great curiosity in those parts" (*Mendip Annals,* 12). The gorge still attracts many tourists today. (Image courtesy of National Trust, UK.)

William Wilberforce by Karl Anton Hickel, c. 1784. Wilberforce encouraged Hannah More, "Call on me for money without reserve. Everyone should contribute out of his own proper fund. I have more money than time, and if you or your sister will condescend to be my almoner, you will enable me to employ some of the superfluity it has pleased God to give me to good purpose. Besides, I have a rich banker in London, Mr. Henry Thornton . . ."

their orchards and poaching their rabbits. The children, she argued, would be involved in nobler pursuits, like learning to read.

That fall of 1789, Hannah and her energetic sister Patty visited the town of Cheddar, famous for its impressive gorge and cheeses. They found the impoverished village languishing, with about two hundred houses and just over one thousand inhabitants. Most of the adults and children worked on farms, although some of the women worked at the paper mill or were employed in knitting and spinning. The More sisters found the farmers remarkably ignorant, often drunk, and spiritually underserved. The vicar spent most of his time in Oxford and rarely visited.[8]

Hannah and Patty bravely visited these "poor, ignorant, and miserable" people in their kitchens and public houses (pubs) to advertise the sisters' intentions to set up a school. They saw "more ignorance than we supposed existed anywhere in England." The only Bible they observed was propping up a flowerpot. Referring to missionary endeavors in Africa, Hannah described her work in the Mendip Hills as "my own little Sierra Leone." (For more stories of the sisters' adventures in the region, see Patty's journal, *The Mendip Annals*.)

Hannah and Patty knew they would need the support of the local clergy in each village if they were to find a building in which to open a school. In Bristol, the mother of a vicar who was friendly with Charles Wesley recommended the first teacher in Cheddar, a widow named Sarah Baber. Hannah knew the "methodistic" teachers were best at Sunday school instruction because they had read their Bibles. In addition, Mrs. Baber was suitably evangelical. However, Hannah had to assure the clergy that neither she nor Mrs. Baber had departed from the Church of England, despite the anxiety among certain Anglicans over the so-called "nonconformists." Of course, the sisters knew that Wilberforce, himself a supporter of the new Sunday School Society pioneered by Robert Raikes, was eager to provide the children in the countryside with the Christian nurturing and morality associated with learning to read the Holy Bible.

Five weeks after the Cheddar school opened on October 25, 1789, Hannah wrote to Wilberforce that thirty pupils said their catechism

---

8 The vicar, or rector, was the clergyman in charge of a chapel and overseer of a parish in the Church of England. He often lived more comfortably outside his assigned parish. The curate, a clergyman often younger and on a lower rung, most often conducted the services.

On October 25, 1789, the More sisters opened their first school with 140 children "with exhortations, portions of Scripture and prayer" (*Mendip Annals*, 23). (Photos courtesy of William Phemister.)

correctly and forty could sing three psalms. The children learned about cleanliness, decency, and honesty. She reported that even the most rowdy, hard-boiled youngsters came week after week to learn to read. Little by little, the word spread, and as soon as the sisters could find suitable teachers, they opened schools in neighboring localities. Some farmers now began to see the advantages of the new schools and Sunday schools. Their tenants' children behaved better.

Robert Raikes (1725–1811) of Gloucester is credited with starting the Sunday school movement in general, but his schools for poor children had not reached the mining communities in the rough West Country of England. That was Hannah's challenge.

Hannah and Patty soon established cooperative women's clubs patterned on the already existing men's societies. The poor women in the area contributed a few pence each month and found a venue where they could socialize and exchange recipes on how to get the most from potatoes and cheap cuts of meat. They also started a communal fund to meet special needs. The members especially appreciated the fact that money from the club could be tapped for their own decent burial, a high value benefit. The More sisters also encouraged the wealthier residents of the manor houses to contribute to these societies for the common good.

Robert Raikes (1725–1811) was an English newspaperman and evangelical Anglican, noted for his promotion of Sunday schools. Raikes was concerned about the effect of the Industrial Revolution upon children, especially boys. The youngsters worked long hours and had no means of moral, religious, or educational development. Most of their parents were illiterate. Raikes used his paper, the *Gloucester Journal,* to publicize the schools and used laypeople to teach reading and writing, using the Bible as the textbook. By 1831, Sunday schools in Great Britain taught 1,250,000 children, approximately 25 percent of the population. They are seen as the forerunners of the current English school system. In America, the first Sunday schools started in the 1790s and followed the Raikes model. (Image courtesy of Gloucester Civic Trust.)

As Hannah listened to the women, she learned with dismay that the loaves of bread sent to the poor in the country were underweight compared to the bread for sale in Bristol, Bath, and other larger towns. In a letter Hannah wrote to Mrs. Garrick, she reported that she had visited magistrates and justices in forty parishes to right these injustices. Hannah constantly worked for the poor; later, when her earnings from her writings increased, she often contributed her own money for their relief. In addition, she knitted white stockings for the graduating girls who had plans for

Sarah Trimmer (1741–1810), painted by Henry Howard. Robert Raikes also inspired Sarah Trimmer to become active in the Sunday school movement. In addition, she founded charity schools in her neighborhood (Brentford) and authored textbooks and stories for children, as well as teaching manuals. She may be best known for *The Guardian of Education,* a periodical in which she reviewed children's books. Her efforts inspired other women such as Hannah More to write for children and the poor. Trimmer and her husband had twelve children. (Image courtesy of the Ealing Local History Center.)

marriage. Her London Bluestocking friends who could knit also pitched in and contributed their handmade white stockings for the young girls.

Hannah and Patty continued to advise these communities on how to work together to form joint ventures. They encouraged a village to build a central oven for baking breads and rice puddings, to buy a cow and share the milk for their babies, and to make butter to sell for a profit. The Mores begged the landowners to permit their workers to plant greens and vegetables for better nutrition at the corners of their fields, and they urged them to buy rice in bulk so the gentry could resell it to the poorer folks, without profit. They also instituted evening prayers in the almshouses for the poor and used their own resources to provide food and clothing for the destitute.

Familiarly known as the Hannah More Clubs, the community associations continued to exist until the twentieth century. The final meeting of the Cheddar Club was held on April 30, 1951. At that time, about £800 was distributed to the remaining ninety-five members. The evening closed with a singing of "Auld Lang Syne." As the club disbanded, the local vicar remembered Hannah's work, calling her "the Great Lady."[9] These women's clubs had a unique welfare function no other organization at the time matched.

Encouraged by the success of the Cheddar school and those in nearby Shipham and Rowberrow, the Mores started and promoted schools at Axbridge, Nailsea, Barley Wood, Wedmore, Yatton, Blagdon, and Congresbury. Unforeseen troubles with the clergy at the school in Blagdon soon emerged. These difficulties became known collectively as "The Blagdon Controversy" and are addressed in the next chapter.

Shipham, in the heart of the mining country, offered stiff challenges to the More sisters. In a 1915 account, "The Heart of Mendip," Francis A. Knight reported the "most interesting figure in the history of Shipham

---

9   Somerset Heritage Centre papers. DA-95438

St. Leonard's Church, Shipham, Somerset, England, sits on a thirteenth-century foundation and was rebuilt in 1842. The two stained-glass windows behind the baptismal font depict two early Christian women, Dorcas and Phoebe. The windows were given in memory of Hannah More. A memorial tablet located near the pulpit and written by Hannah More honors the Reverend James Jones, who assisted her in her work. (Image courtesy of William Phemister.)

The Mendip Hills (commonly called the Mendips) are a range of limestone hills to the south of Bristol and Bath in Somerset, England. The quarries were major suppliers for stone to build the cities of Bath and Bristol and the road stone for southern England. Underground caves and rivers now make the area a center for caving. The Cheddar Gorge is an example of the many scenic attractions for modern tourists. (Image courtesy of Somerset Tourism.)

is that of Hannah More, who with her sister Martha (Patty to her family), did so much for the poor and ignorant and neglected people of this district, in the closing years of the eighteenth century." The inhabitants mined lead, zinc, and calamine, and were notorious for their rough manners and lawless lives. The old rector at the time lived a long way from Shipham, where "it is said he had not preached a sermon or baptized a child for forty years" (Knight, 145).

To emphasize further the lawlessness of the area at the time when the More sisters began their philanthropic labors, Knight wrote that "no constable dared venture into the village to arrest a man for fear that he should be made away with, thrown down some old mine shaft, and never heard from again." The population in 1790 was 772, and by 1911 it had dwindled to 359. Hannah wrote of Shipham (as quoted in Knight, 146): "Among the most depraved and wretched were Shipham and Rowberrow, two mining villages on the top of Mendip: the people savage and depraved even beyond Cheddar, brutal in their natures, and ferocious in their manners. They began by suspecting that we should make our fortune by selling their children as slaves."

Gradually, a ray of light began to flicker in the darkness at Shipham. The old rector allowed Hannah to use the vacant rectory for her new school. In September 1790, the Sunday and Day School for the united parishes of Shipham and Rowberrow opened with 140 "scholars." By the spring of 1793, nine hundred children attended the annual celebratory feast; also in attendance were farmers and their wives, who brought the number to seven thousand. Feeding such a large group became a major annual undertaking that Hannah willingly undertook.

Girls who attended the schools received special attention. Those who continued in instruction until they reached a certain age or married, and who had maintained a good character, were presented at the feast with five shillings, a customary pair of white stockings, and a new Bible. Hannah deeply believed in the importance of female education, but opportunities for girls were sadly lacking in England up to that time. Canadian literary scholar Claire Crogan adds, "Without the least intending it, devout women like More and Trimmer mapped out new female fields, playing within the rules of the game, yet underneath reworking the female sphere of autonomy, through moral reform, sexual complementarity, and freedom from sexual exploitation" (Crogan, 209).

George IV (1762–1830). From 1811 until his accession to the throne ten years later, he served as prince regent during his father's final mental illness. His title gave the label to the period known as the Regency Period. His ministers found his behavior selfish, wasteful in time of war, and irresponsible. Hannah More, William Wilberforce, and others found his behavior reprehensible and wrote against his dissipations.

CHAPTER 7

FOREVER LINKED WITH WILBERFORCE AND THE ABOLITION OF THE SLAVERY IN ENGLAND

"We have employments assigned to us for every circumstance in life. When we are alone, we have our thoughts to watch; in the family, our tempers; and in company, our tongues."

After Hannah met William Wilberforce at Bath in 1786, she described him to her Bluestocking friend Elizabeth Carter as a young man with apostolic zeal. His quick wit, charm, sense of humor, and commitment to his two major callings in life attracted her immediately. He was slight of build and fourteen years younger than Hannah, but his powers of oratory gave him an immense stature among his friends and even his enemies in Parliament. She shared his abhorrence of the slave trade and his dedication to working for significant societal reforms. In February 1787, Hannah lent her voice to his campaign by publishing her lengthy poem "Slavery" to coincide with Wilberforce's first parliamentary debate on the slave trade. Lines 251–254:

> *Shall Britain, where the soul of Freedom reigns*
> *Forge chains for others she herself disdains?*
> *Forbid it Heaven! O let the nations know*
> *The liberty she loves she will bestow.*

Eighteenth-century England was known for lewd and disorderly conduct. Gambling, drunkenness, prostitution, cursing, and petty crime reigned. In a short period of time, a determined Wilberforce launched a vigorous effort to mobilize the country's leadership against vice. Both he and Hannah felt that the king and nobility should set the standards for moral conduct by acting upon Christian principles. Good behavior and Sabbath-keeping would then trickle down to the lower classes. Wilberforce also worked with the Bishop of London, the Right Reverend Father Bielby Porteus, for the formation of a Society for the Reformation of Manners. In October 1787, Wilberforce wrote in his diary, "God Almighty has set before me *two great objects,* the suppression of the slave trade and the reformation of manners [morality]" (quoted in Wolffe, 160).

In 1788, Hannah anonymously published *Thoughts on the Importance of Manners of the Great to General Society.* The impact was all the stronger because no one knew who had published it. Many thought it to be Wilberforce. In it, she criticized the rich for their Sunday games and card-playing parties. Fashionable women needed their elaborate coiffeurs arranged in the mornings. Their ladies' maids and other servants could not take Sunday off. To make matters worse, they would not be given another compensating day off later in the week. Coachmen and valets also were required to stand by. In addition, shooting parties and card playing kept the nobility and gentry as well as the servants from going to church on those days. There was frequently no Sabbath rest.

The years spanning the American War for Independence and the Napoleonic Wars were times of great turbulence in Great Britain. King George III was declared mad. His son, George IV, the prince regent, was next in line to the throne and was declared the ruler, but he was not crowned king until 1821. George IV lived a life of loose morals and extravagance and darkened the prestige of the monarchy. Some historians have referred to this time—the Regency Period—as the apex of English decadence.

In *Manners of the Great to General Society,* Hannah bravely took on the heavy gambling, drunkenness, gluttony, lax attitude toward the paying of

---

William Cowper (1731–1800) is best known for the phrase "God moves in mysterious ways, His wonders to perform." Cowper was the most popular poet of his time. Hannah said of him, "I am enchanted with this poet; his images [are] so natural and so much his own! Such an original and philosophic thinker!" Later she wrote to a friend, "I have found what I have been looking for all my life, a poet whom I can read on Sunday." Hannah was well-known as a strict observer of the Sabbath.

---

debts, and degenerate attitude toward women that she saw among some of the aristocracy. The book went through seven editions within a few months.

There was more to Hannah More's treatise than just reminding the rich and the royals to mind their Sabbath etiquette. To both More and Wilberforce, the reformation of manners addressed the decline of Christian moral behavior among the upper classes and the prevalent social evils in their time. They wanted to bring Christian spirituality back to Great Britain. They strove to impress upon the upper classes their special role as the moral beacons of society—the lighthouses on the hills. She wrote, "Mischief arises not from our living in the world, but from the world living in us" (*Manners*, 68).

Hannah continued to make her annual trips to London, staying with Mrs. Garrick. However, now as a spiritual seeker, she carried a strong desire for more spiritual depth in her life. She sought out the Reverend John Newton, the former slave ship captain. She had read his autobiography, *An Authentic Narrative,* which described his religious conversion and how he had worked hard to educate himself to become an ordained Anglican clergyman. He described his first appointment to the small market town of Olney and how he came to meet the evangelical poet and hymn writer William Cowper. The two men later collaborated on *Olney Hymns* (1779). Then came Newton's appointment to a more prestigious church in

AMAZING GRACE !
HOW SWEET THE SOUND
JOHN NEWTON

To the Glory of God & in loving memory of
ARCHIBALD ALLEN
for many years solicitor in this town
and his wife EMILY MAUD ALLEN
Their daughter Evelyn Gaskard Allen caused this
and the window opposite to be installed A.D 1927

John Newton (1725–1807) pictured in the "Amazing Grace" window at Olney Church. The Reverend John Newton was also a spiritual mentor to William Wilberforce and his ally in the abolitionist cause. In 1784, he advised the twenty-four-year-old Member of Parliament not to withdraw from political life but to stay in the House of Commons and serve God as a Christian statesman. Consider the implications if young William Wilberforce had quit politics; it would have been a huge defeat to his resolve to abolish the slave trade, a law that only the government could enact. (Photo courtesy of William Phemister.)

London, St. Mary Woolnoth. Here, in 1787, Hannah could finally meet the man who had found God's grace so very amazing in his life.

John Newton's significant influence on Hannah's life steered her in the direction of distinctive Christian service, philanthropy, and identifying herself as an evangelical. Consequently, Hannah, one of the most influential women of her generation and part of the prestigious Samuel Johnson circle, slowly began to grow discontented with London's fashionable social scene.

The abolitionist movement had begun earlier in the century with the Quakers and the Wesley brothers, John (1703–1791) and Charles (1707–1788). Before then, few had questioned the immorality of owning slaves. Leading Christians of high rank now began to reason that slavery, although presumed in the Bible, was inconsistent not only with Christianity but also with common justice and human rights. It was morally wrong to make slaves of other human beings, made in the image of God, against their will.

While Hannah was enjoying a certain stature at the height of her London triumph as a playwright and as a member of the Bluestockings,

Charles Wesley sent her a letter of encouragement. An abolitionist himself, he advised her to remain in the fashionable world, where she could influence the great and noble. He reasoned that she had much to contribute to the moral health of society. Later, because of her friendship with the Wesleys, Hannah would be accused by her enemies of being "too methodistic," that is, showing too much enthusiasm for social reform based on her Christian convictions.

Any religious or emotional fervor in the minds of some people was linked to revolutionary discontent or political upheaval. "Methodism," to some Church of England adherents, became a scapegoat for the revolutions occurring in America (1776) and France (1789). However, Hannah, along with George Whitefield and John and Charles Wesley—the principal people accused of founding this new "religious hysteria"—never left the Anglican Church. Rodney Stark, in his *For the Glory of God,* suggests that probably the only reason these evangelicals did not leave the Church of England was that, at this time, only members of the Church of England had full civil rights, including the exclusive right to serve in the House of Commons (Stark, 239).

St. Mary Woolnoth is an Anglican church in London and has been used for Christian worship for at least a thousand years. The name "Woolnoth" refers to a benefactor, possibly one Wulnoth de Walebrok, known to have lived in the area in the twelfth century. The building was badly damaged in 1666 during the Great Fire of London but repaired by Sir Christopher Wren. Hannah More and William Wilberforce worshiped at St. Mary Woolnoth while the Reverend John Newton was the rector (1780–1807). (Photo courtesy of London Tourist Information.)

John Wesley often spoke against the slave trade, calling it "this infernal traffic" (in Anstey, *Atlantic Slave Trade*, 240). Hannah became strongly influenced by a number of Anglican clergymen during this time, not only by John and Charles Wesley and John Newton, but also by Thomas Scott, Newton's successor in London, and by the Right Reverend Bielby Porteus, Bishop of London, to mention a few. Hannah spoke out more as the movement gained momentum; she joined those who boycotted sugar to protest the slave plantations where the sugarcane was grown. Later, as she established her Sunday schools in the Mendip Hills and encountered dispiriting opposition, she would call on the help of her many clergy friends, including the bishops in Bristol, Bath, London, and Wells in particular. They all recognized her exemplary work in social reform.

Through Wilberforce and others in the evangelical movement in the Church of England, Hannah came in contact with the fellowship known, after the death of Wilberforce, as the Clapham Sect. This circle of men and women took their name from the group of mostly wealthy businessmen who gathered from time to time in the large home of Henry Thornton. His spacious home faced the Clapham Common at Battersea Rise, just south of the city of London. The Thornton house was demolished, but St. Paul's Church, where Henry Thornton is buried, still stands. This area, formerly south of London, is now incorporated into London proper.

Later, when Hannah was writing to a larger audience in her popular *Cheap Repository Tracts,* she included the ballad, "The Sorrows of Yamba;

John Wesley (1703–1791), pictured three days before his death, is writing his famous letter to Wilberforce in which he concluded, "Unless God has raised you up for this very thing, you will be worn out by the opposition of men and devils. But if God be for you, who can be against you?" (Image reprinted from A.B. Hyde, *The Story of Methodism Throughout the World,* MA: Willy & Co., 1889. Used by permission of Photos.com.)

Olaudah Equiano (1745–1797) was an African befriended and supported by abolitionists such as William Wilberforce, Henry Thornton, and Granville Sharp. All encouraged him to write his autobiography. *The Interesting Narrative of the Life of Olaudah Equiano,* first published in 1789, depicted the horrors of slavery and influenced the enactment of the Slave Trade Act of 1807. According to his account, he was born in Nigeria and later bought by Michael Pascal, a lieutenant in the Royal Navy, who renamed him Gustavus Vassa. Scholars disagree about Equiano's origins, citing baptismal records in South Carolina, but all agree that his book fueled the growing antislavery movement in Great Britain. Equiano became a Methodist, having been influenced by George Whitefield's evangelism during what is known in America as the Great Awakening.

or, The Negro Woman's Lamentation," written with Eaglesfield Smith. The emotion used in this poem focuses on the maltreatment of slaves forcefully removed from Africa and herded onto slave ships like cattle. The poem describes a Negro woman's separation from her child. The child mercifully dies on board the ship, never to feel the cruel whip:

> Happy, happy there she lies
> Thou shalt feel the lash no more.
> Thus full many a Negro dies
> E're we reach the destin'd shore.

Hannah was not afraid to advance her political agenda based on her Christian belief that slavery was morally evil, but she had to wait until 1807 for Parliament finally to pass the Slave Trade Act. It came only after much opposition from wealthy merchants who for years had bought off the vote of many parliamentarians. This Act did not mean that the buying, selling, and keeping of slaves was abolished, only that the shipping of slaves from Africa to the colonies ended. Hannah continued to oppose

Original edition of *Sorrows of Yamba*. Used by permission of Bristol City Council.

The great pottery maker, Josiah Wedgwood, joined the abolitionist cause and produced this celebrated medallion depicting a kneeling slave pleading, "Am I not a man and a brother?" Thousands of copies were made, making it a symbol of the abolitionist campaign. Some fashionable ladies wore facsimiles in their hair; some gentlemen had them inlaid onto the top of their snuff boxes (Hague, 150). (Image used courtesy of the British Museum.)

slavery throughout her life, but by 1807, her health was failing, and she was not able to play as active a role as she had earlier.

Slavery itself in Great Britain was not abolished until 1833. William Wilberforce received the news on his deathbed in July. Hannah died later the same year, September 6, 1833. Happily, they both lived to see the success of their hard-won fight, which remains an outstanding milestone in British humanitarian history. More gave full credit to her lifelong friend Wilberforce, but she courageously did her part—all that was possible for an activist woman to do in those days. Hannah More remains a forward-looking model, a necessary precondition, for the women's rights that came later. (Women in Great Britain did not receive the vote until 1918. In the United States, the vote was won two years later, in 1920.)

In a somewhat surprisingly satirical essay, "The White Slave Trade," written in the 1790s, Hannah took the metaphor of slavery to attempt, by parody, to liberate the women of London and Westminster from the demands of "fashion." She blamed the often-painful strictures of body shape and style imposed on young women during courtship and marriage of being a kind of slavery. She viewed such restrictive, voguish styles as akin to slave auction markets. This mock discourse was aimed

Slavery was not abolished in the United States until President Abraham Lincoln (1809–1865) delivered the Emancipation Proclamation on January 1, 1863. The proclamation later became the Thirteenth Amendment to the US Constitution. (Image courtesy of Photos.com)

at emancipating women from the imposed bondage of "white slavery." She hoped to heighten the consciousness of women to reflect on their own self-imposed captivity. If women perpetuated superficial, shallow accomplishments rather than seeking a solid education and their true selves, they were accomplices in their own bondage. Hannah wanted to set women free from the binding preoccupation with self and culture's distorted view of beauty. She knew women's worth came from being created in God's image, not from an imposed, stylized body shape.

Hannah More came to London a stranger, a plain schoolmistress from Bristol, and yet in an impressively short time she became one of the best-known and most charismatic leaders in the ranks of the growing evangelical movement. Her name will be linked forever with William Wilberforce and the abolition of slavery, the founding of schools for the poor, the wearing of comfortable clothing, and the promotion of Christian ideals for the good of England.

Hannah More and William Wilberforce were featured on the face of stamps issued in Great Britain in 2007 to commemorate the passage of the Slave Trade Act of 1807. (Images courtesy of Philatelia.net.)

~

CHAPTER 8

WHEN HELPING OTHERS TURNS OUT BADLY
The Blagdon Controversy

"O, Jealousy, thou ugliest fiend of hell! Thy deadly venom preys on my vitals, turns the healthful hue of my fresh cheek to haggard sallowness, and drinks my spirit up."

The struggle between the evangelical branch of the Church of England, which favored Sunday schools, and the conservative faction which considered More's schools to be dangerous Methodist propaganda, came to be known as "The Blagdon Controversy" (1799–1803). Hannah's friends and financial backers at Battersea Rise—William Wilberforce, Henry Thornton, Zachary Macaulay, and others who were part of the Clapham Group—increasingly influenced and encouraged Hannah in her work. (The term "Clapham Sect" was coined only after Wilberforce's death. *Sect* implies a deviant theology, an accusative charge that erroneously stuck to this group of reformers.) As noted, the Reverends John and Charles Wesley and George Whitefield had influenced the Clapham legislators to act on the moral convictions of their Christian faith.

Patty recorded in her journal that on the first Sunday that Henry Thornton came to Cowslip Green for a visit, Patty and Hannah took their benefactor to visit their schools in Shipham, Axbridge, and Cheddar. On the following Sunday, they visited Yatton and Nailsea. "Mr. Thornton went over

Henry Thornton (1760–1815) was an English banker, economist, philanthropist, abolitionist, and independent Member of Parliament. He refused to bribe people the standard two guineas for their votes, becoming a man respected for his morals and integrity. He became a major player in the establishment of the Sierra Leone Company, organized to set up a settlement for freed slaves in Africa. Thornton also assisted Hannah More in the publishing and writing of the *Cheap Repository Tracts*. His eldest child, Marianne (given the same name as her mother, who was also a Bluestocking), became a good friend of Hannah's.

to the poorhouse, and found a dreadful scene of neglect, misery, and ignorance" (*Mendip Annals*, 166). Before long, this traveling party of women and notables had a deputation from the village of Blagdon accompanying them. Mr. Bere, the curate, petitioned them to do *his* parish some good as well. All started well in Blagdon, but the effort was to end miserably for Hannah and her sisters.

The school at Blagdon opened in 1795, in the same manner as the other schools—first by gaining the approval of the local clergy (including Mr. Bere) and then by finding a suitable teacher. Things went along

Today, the village of Blagdon claims a Hannah More House on Church Street, privately owned, where "social reformer Hannah More once used the house as a schoolroom." Any controversy involving Mr. Bere is not mentioned, nor does he have a plaque commemorating his stay in the village. (Photo courtesy English Heritage Explorer.)

fine until 1798, when the at-first amiable Mr. Bere preached a sermon criticizing the school. He also accused Hannah of knowingly employing a Methodist teacher and having "methodistical enthusiasm" herself. The Church of England regarded the growth of Methodism and its "enthusiasm" with apprehension.

In the eighteenth century, *enthusiasm*, according to Dr. Johnson's famous *Dictionary* (the first comprehensive dictionary in the English language), was defined as "a *vain* belief of private revelation; a *vain* confidence of divine favour" (italics mine). In contemporary usage, the word simply means intense enjoyment, interest, or approval. Following the English Civil War in the previous century (1642–1651), *enthusiasm* was a pejorative term for support of any new political or religious cause. "Methodists" such as the aforementioned John Wesley or George Whitefield were accused of *enthusiasm* (i.e., fanaticism and arrogance). They defended themselves by distinguishing fanaticism from what they termed "religion of the heart."

This dispute in Blagdon gave rise to twenty-three pamphlets written by one side or the other. The mildest accused Hannah of knowingly employing the "enthusiast" schoolmaster Henry Young. The biting critic William Cobbett, as cited in the prologue, called her "a she-bishop in petticoats!" She, in turn, accused the Reverend Mr. Bere of preaching against the Trinity and denying the divinity of Jesus. She refused to dismiss the teacher, and consequently she was disparaged by some as a seditious radical.

Continuous, vicious attacks in the press wore on her and left Hannah dispirited. During this especially heated time of name-calling and derision, her friends Wilberforce and Thornton were away in Bognor, on the south coast of England, where Mrs. Wilberforce was recovering from typhoid fever, a life-threatening disease. Hannah's own rector in Wrington kept his head down and stayed out of the fray. She felt abandoned. The disagreement escalated into what some of her friends called "The Blagdon Persecution."

Moreover, during this troublesome time, her good friend Elizabeth
Montagu died. Mrs. Montagu had been a true friend, a generous contributor
to Hannah's charities, and an understanding ally during the Ann Yearsley matter. This severed link from her Bluestocking past felt like an ampu-
tation. It seemed that her friends had left her at her time of greatest need.
Hannah wrote to Wilberforce, "I cannot command my nerves . . . I get
disturbed and agitated at night" (Yonge, 134).

The accusations against Hannah alleged that the schoolmaster she
had hired was "a Methodist and a Calvinist; that he ran secret meetings;
that he called the clergy dumb dogs; that he and members of his little
group prayed extempore, and that he prayed for the French" (Stott, 236).
The chancellor, the person in the Church of England who assigns the
clergy, wrote an order to dismiss the schoolmaster. Some of the clergy,
friends of the Reverend Mr. Bere, closed ranks against this lone woman
who wanted only to educate the children in their parishes.

Hannah felt the school was lost to her. She appealed to Reverend
Bere's rector, the absent Dr. George Crossman, who was already receiving reports of his curate's unorthodoxy. As a result, the Blagdon School
closed and never reopened. In February 1801, Reverend Bere received formal notification that he was no longer curate. Although devastated, he
remained the curate in a neighboring village; he was not left destitute.
Another post in Ireland turned up for the controversial young schoolmaster, Mr. Young, and his wife.

After the whole matter was settled, the Mendip clergy lined up, some
on Reverend Bere's side, most on Hannah's. The high church journal
British Critic supported her, as did Bishop Porteus of London, but now
the controversy was public property. The hullabaloo became a significant
moment, not only for Hannah but also for the Church of England. Many
lords and ladies who knew Hannah backed her; the conservative church
people backed Mr. Bere. Hannah barely survived the ordeal.

From 1803 to 1805, Hannah succumbed to what she referred to as "my
great illness." To modern readers, it looks like a major case of depression.

Bielby Porteus, Bishop of London (1731–1809). The Right Reverend Bielby Porteus was the first Anglican in a position of authority to challenge the church's position on slavery. He was a friend of Wilberforce, Hannah More, and the Clapham Sect of "revolutionary" social reformers. Well known as a passionate advocate of personal Bible reading and a founding member of the British and Foreign Bible Society, he worked with Methodists and dissenters, recognizing their major contributions to evangelism and education.

She lost confidence in herself and seemed listless, requiring her worried sisters to stay with her for the entire winter. Ten years later, she wrote to Wilberforce, "In that long affliction I very seldom closed my eyes for forty days and nights" (Roberts, vol. III, 243). Patty, especially, was frantic over Hannah's illnesses, but to the surprise of Hannah's surviving friends, she lived into her eighty-ninth year, another twenty-eight years.

Though some of the schools failed, others continued. By 1840, they had become national schools. In the twentieth century, these backcountry schools for the poor, like the Sunday schools of Robert Raikes, were absorbed into the state system. Hannah and Patty had done the hard work that paved the way for something far greater. "Her truly valuable legacy," wrote biographer Charlotte Mary Yonge, "was not only the example of what one woman could be, and could do, but a real influence on the tone of education in all classes of English women" (196).

Hannah More Infants' School in Nailsea, near Bristol. Hannah More's name is still remembered in modern Somerset County. (Photo courtesy of William Phemister.)

Barley Wood, just a mile on the other side of Wrington, was situated on a high piece of land with a view sloping down to the Bristol Channel. The house was two stories high, built of stone, and crowned with a thatched roof. A rustic veranda with a trellis around the first story soon became draped with honeysuckle, jasmine, woodbine, and clematis. The sisters never tired of improving the grounds, planting lovely larch, laurel, chestnut, and other trees and shrubs. (Photo courtesy of William Phemister.)

CHAPTER 9

THE MAGNET OF BARLEY WOOD

"A Christian will find it cheaper to pardon than to resent. Forgiveness saves the expense of anger, the cost of hatred, the waste of spirits."

By the turn of the century, Hannah's one-story thatched cottage in the country, Cowslip Green, had become too small. With many friends and sponsors of her schools coming to visit—the Wilberforces, the Macaulays, and the Thorntons, to name a few—she had trouble packing them in. Moreover, the little house could not be properly heated for cold weather. Lying in a valley, it was prone to unhealthy, piercing dampness. To minimize her often-feverish bouts of ague, Hannah spent the cold winter months in London with Mrs. Garrick or in Bath on Pulteney Street with her sisters until her new home became livable.

In 1802, Mrs. More moved one mile from Cowslip Green to Barley Wood, the house she had built on higher ground but still in the village of Wrington, Somerset County. Soon afterward, her sisters disposed of their house in Bath and came to live with her. For the next twenty years, friends of all ages and from all ranks came to visit Hannah and her sisters, seeking advice, sympathy, and assistance. At sixty-three, she was now politely referred to as Mrs. More, although she and her sisters never married.

Hannah More's immense correspondence occupied a large portion of her time. Her gifted ability to communicate to all levels of the social

LOCKE'S URN, BARLEY WOOD.

Locke's Urn, Barley Wood. The great philosopher John Locke (1632–1704), who wrote *Two Treatises of Government* (which influenced Thomas Jefferson in the writing of the Declaration of Independence), was born in Wrington over a century before Hannah More was born. Elizabeth Montagu knew of Hannah's admiration for Locke's views on education, which had influenced her own practice when she set up her Sunday schools, and in 1791 presented her with this urn inscribed:

To John Locke,
This memorial is executed by Mrs. Montagu
and presented to Hannah More.

Hannah took it with her when she moved to Barley Wood, and it became a feature on the grounds long after her death. Its whereabouts now are unknown. (Sketch by Henry Thompson, originally in *Life of Hannah More.)*

spectrum contributed to her immense success. Still, she was not free from troublesome stress or from the long attacks of illness that she endured with long-suffering grace. The ripples of the Blagdon Controversy continued to widen with accusations over what some called her "Methodism" and her alleged subversive religious and political involvements. Yet, despite the repeated health challenges and resulting depression, she persisted in writing about what concerned her most: the education of the poor and the improvement of the morals and religious conviction among

PORTEUS'S URN, BARLEY WOOD.

Porteus's Urn, Barley Wood. The Bishop of London, the Right Reverend Bielby Porteus, died in May 1809 and left Hannah £200 in stock; she set up this urn at Barley Wood, "In Memory of Long and Faithful Friendship." Although the bishop had never formally identified himself with the evangelicals, at his death, she had lost her chief supporter on the Episcopal bench. (Sketch by Henry Thompson, originally in *Life of Hannah More*.)

the rich. If her critics only knew how her newfound religious sensibilities would energize her determination to right the wrongs in her world as she saw them!

Cœlebs in Search of a Wife was written at Barley Wood and was soon followed by *Practical Piety, or the Influence of Religion of the Heart on the Conduct of Life* (1811). It quickly sold out and then ran to ten editions. Hannah's biographer, Mary Alden Hopkins, records that two Persian gentlemen visiting the author received a copy of the novel from her hands and declared it should be the first book printed on the printing press they were carrying back to their native land. *Practical Piety* was also translated into Icelandic (*Hannah More and Her Circle*, 231–232). A Swiss couple, Francois and Marie-Aimée Huber, kept her informed about the evangelicals in Geneva, and in 1816, they translated *Cœlebs* into French (Stott, 290).

In *Practical Piety*, Hannah records what she learned about herself and God through her sufferings: "The love of reputation begins to mix itself with your better motives . . . It is a delicious poison which begins to infuse itself into your purest cup . . . [if] your fame was too dear to you . . . it must be offered up . . . He makes us feel our weakness, that we may have recourse to His *strength*" (181–4).

As a sequel to this work, she published *Christian Morals* in 1812; this too was widely circulated. Three years later, she wrote an *Essay on the Character and Writings of St. Paul* in two volumes. It was greeted with the same eagerness as her earlier works. Due to her prestige in the evangelical world and despite acknowledging her deficiencies in ancient languages and biblical criticism, the first edition sold out before publication in 1815.

Barley Wood, located fairly close to Bristol and Bath, attracted many visitors who regarded Mrs. More as a kind of high priestess of the evangelical movement. People came from near and far to see this now-famous author, philanthropist, and reformer, as if visiting a shrine. The well-known romantic poet Samuel Taylor Coleridge dropped in for a social call in 1814 while giving lectures on Shakespeare in Bristol. Earlier, she had

Coleridge in 1795. Samuel Taylor Coleridge (1772–1834) was a founder, along with his friend William Wordsworth (1770–1850), of the Romantic Poets in England, sometimes referred to as the Lake Poets. He is probably best known for his poems "The Rime of the Ancient Mariner" (1798) and "Kubla Khan" (1816).

Although Barley Wood has been a good deal altered since Hannah's time, the general effect has stayed much like the old illustrations. When the author visited the site in 2014, "For Sale" signs were posted at the entrance. The most recent occupants at Barley Wood had been drug reha-

bilitation residents. Peering through the windows of the abandoned structure, it was obvious that much renovation would be needed to make Hannah's former home habitable again. (Photo courtesy of William Phemister.)

avoided Mr. Coleridge due to his deviation into Unitarian theology, but she changed her mind after he had abandoned his radical ideas. During the visit, she noticed his trembling hands, a result of his opium addiction. Laudanum was legal and widely available to treat maladies at that time.

Hannah herself had used morphine to treat her various ailments, but she took solemn warning after seeing Coleridge's symptoms. She also knew that Wilberforce took laudanum, but carefully and under his physician's supervision. In 1816, after an especially demanding time of hosting visitors, Hannah wrote with a sigh to Wilberforce, "The retirement I sought I have never been able to find." (For more of their correspondence, see the William Wilberforce Papers, archived in The Duke University Special Collections Library, Durham, NC.)

Among the many who came to her door was the American educator and clergyman Philander Chase, the first episcopal bishop of Ohio. He wished to create a school in the center of Ohio that would prepare young men for the ministry. (Ohio had become the seventeenth state of the rapidly enlarging United States a mere twenty years earlier, in 1803.) Finding little financial support in his native America, which was quickly pushing westward, he had journeyed across the Atlantic to ask the English for aid. Chase spent several months during the summer of 1824 raising funds for his fledgling school on the American frontier. On July 2, he met with Mrs. More at her Barley Wood home. She must have been persuaded that they had much in common, because she generously contributed to his college, believing it to be a bulwark against nominal Christianity. It is unknown how much money Mrs. More gave him then, but when she died in 1833, she left Bishop Chase £200 for the establishment of Kenyon College in Gambier, Ohio.[10]

---

10 For more information on the Kenyon college connection see
    www.kenyonhistory.net/kcpedia/HannahMore)

Philander Chase (1775–1852), first president of Kenyon College, Gambier, Ohio, first episcopal bishop of Ohio, and later, the first episcopal bishop of Illinois. Because More and Chase shared evangelical beliefs, she contributed generously to his fledgling institute in America. (Image used courtesy of Kenyon College.)

This unusual portrait of Hannah More was painted by Gilbert Stuart (1755–1828) during his visits to the London studio of Sir Joshua Reynolds. Stuart is known for his portrayals of early American presidents and their wives. This portrait of Hannah, long in a private collection, now hangs in the Kenyon College president's office in Gambier, Ohio. In 1969, when the first class of women were admitted to Kenyon College, they named their service group after their early benefac-

tress. A collection of approximately one hundred items of More's writings and many of her letters are housed in the Kenyon College Olin Library Special Collections. (Image courtesy of the Gund Gallery, Kenyon College.)

Modeled by George Cocker after a painting of Miss More by Henry William Pickersgill and made in England at the Derby factory about 1825, this bisque figurine rests behind glass in Kenyon College, Special Collections. (Image courtesy of Kenyon College.)

A copy of the Richard Pickersgill portrait, painted in 1824, shows Hannah More with ruffles and bonnet suitable for a woman of distinction. It was presented to Kenyon College by alumnus Frank H. Ginn and hangs in the Great Hall of the college. The original is in the National Portrait Gallery, London. The Hannah More stamp of Great Britain, appearing in 2007 and on the cover, is

based on the Pickersgill image. (Image courtesy of Kenyon College.)

CHAPTER 10

How Words Prevented
a Revolution

*"Genius without religion is only a lamp on the outer gate
of a palace; it may serve to cast a gleam of light on those that
are without, while the inhabitant sits in darkness."*

I t is difficult to overestimate the influence of Hannah More's *Cheap
Repository Tracts* and her earlier work, *Village Politics,* on quelling the
swiftly moving surge of revolutionary fervor as it swept across France
and now lapped at the shores of England. Some historians hold that this
series of stories, with their accompanying moral applications, actually
stemmed the tide of revolution in England.

After the storming of the Bastille prison and the revolution in France
(1789), Napoleon's armies were on the move. England's long coastline, just
twenty-two miles across the Channel from France, looked like an easy land
grab for Napoleon (1769–1821), who was eager to conquer all of Europe.
France had been at war with Great Britain continuously from 1793 to 1802,
and off and on for years before then.

In France, the Jacobin Clubs had become the most prominent political organizations of the French Revolution in 1789. They first met in a
Dominican convent and became notorious for their fervent support for
the execution of Louis XVI. The Jacobins backed the Reign of Terror that
sent thousands to the guillotine. At the same time, Napoleon's star was
rising in France, and he emerged as a military hero. In 1797, the French

landed a small contingent in South Wales. The invasion failed, but this aggressive action heightened concern regarding Napoleon's plans. That same year he invaded Austria and the following year sailed for Egypt, hoping to destroy British trade with the Middle East and India. He met with disaster when he encountered Lord Nelson and his British sea power. Nevertheless, Napoleon proclaimed victory and returned to France, where the French believed him. In 1804, he crowned himself emperor of France for life. Is it any wonder that the royalists and clergy in Great Britain who saw what was happening in France feared any groups that might be conspiring against the established Church of England or the monarchy?

Inside the Dominican convent on the Rue St. Jacques. The rebellious Jacobin members were not only against the king but were also anticlerical, imprisoning priests and looting churches. The clubs closed soon after Robespierre was killed in 1794, but not before "Jacobinism" became synonymous with revolutionary fervor and fear. The clubs took their name from the street, *Rue St Jacques* (*James* in English; *Jacobus* in Latin).

A new magazine, *The Anti-Jacobin,* started up in London to discredit the radical political values of the French Revolution. To some in that day, "Jacobinism" stirred up the same emotional fervor as the words "Socialism" or "Communism" do in the United States today.

The children and adults who had learned to read their Bibles in the More sisters' schools were now able to some extent to read Thomas Paine and *The Rights of Man.* The revolutionary writings of Paine and William Godwin (founder of philosophical anarchism) aroused alarm in the minds of the comfortable upper and middle classes. The words *liberty*

Napoleon Crossing the Alps, the famous painting by Jacques-Louis David. Needing money for his war, Napoleon Bonaparte sold France's North American possessions in the United States—the Louisiana Purchase—for less than three cents per acre. He also reestablished slavery in France's colonial possessions, which had been banned following the French Revolution of 1789.

and *equality,* wafting over the channel from France, dazzled the farmers and factory workers.

Hannah's good friend the Bishop of London, Beilby Porteus, begged her to write something in easy-to-understand English for her new readers—something that would reassure the uneducated that the English already had the blessings and protections in their government that the French had revolted to achieve. At first she demurred, but as she lay in bed recovering from grave illness, she wrote her first tract: *Village Politics Addressed to all the Mechanics, Journeymen and Day Labourers in Great Britain, by Will Chip, a Country Carpenter* (1793).

Frontispiece of *Village Politics.*

She designed the short, popular tract, written anonymously, to counter the arguments of Thomas Paine's popular tract, *The Rights of Man,* which had sharpened the appetite among the poor for political reform. In plain English, *Village Politics* is a dialogue between a blacksmith, Jack, and a mason, Tom. Jack points out to Tom, who has gotten his hands on a copy of *The Rights of Man,* that the English already enjoy the tried-and-true British political system, complete with a constitution. Unlike the French, who had whipped themselves into mob furies and had killed their king and his family, Englishmen, Hannah wrote, enjoyed the protection of the law. If Tom the mason should fall upon hard times, poor working men like himself could find help from the religious or private charities already existing in England. Fomenting a revolution would just bring pandemonium to their stable country.

More's beliefs were conservative and hierarchical, consistent with her times. She believed one must be loyal to "Caesar," but in her *ideal* society, people would learn to be *inter*dependent, finding respite and happiness in what she believed to be the traditional Christian order of things. Hannah, along with Edmund Burke, the dominant political thinker of the day, who also happened to represent her district in Parliament, often reflected and

Frontispiece of *The Contented Cobbler,* an example of a Cheap Repository Tract, the name given to the series of religious and political tracts published between March 1795 and December 1797 for sale or distribution to the poor. They became extremely successful. It is estimated that two million were printed up each year. Published on inexpensive paper, the stories were twelve or twenty-four pages long, printed up in a format similar to chapbooks. Chapbooks had been popular in the seventeenth century; they were little pocket-sized booklets on cheap paper containing poetry, illustrations, nursery rhymes, bawdy ballads, and political messages, sold by peddlers in rural areas. Hannah More's *Cheap Repository Tracts* became much more entertaining and widespread and sold rapidly.

spoke on the dire consequences that would follow the mismanagement of change. (The More sisters had worked for Burke's election.) They did not want to see repeated in England the chaos that had happened in France.

Village Politics was translated into French, Italian, and Welsh, and it became so successful that Bishop Porteus and members of the Clapham Group looked for additional ways to produce readable moral tales. Again, they looked to Hannah. Bishop Porteus, especially, admired her writing. He also knew from her work with charity and Sunday schools among the poor that she knew her audience well and could relate to its speech patterns. In addition, he knew that Hannah's patriotism and morality were highly respected among the highbrow circles in London in which she circulated. The wealthy would underwrite her tracts with paid subscriptions. The gentry and aristocrats did in fact purchase numerous copies for a half-penny a piece for distribution among their friends, workers, and in public houses, much as free materials are placed in stores today. They scattered the tracts like wind-blown seeds across the land. Keeping their workers calm and submissive with reading material of moral worth served not only to benefit themselves but also to preserve a more peaceful nation.

From 1795 to 1797, Hannah produced her *Cheap Repository Tracts* at the rate of three a month. They poured from her pen like torrents in springtime. Translated into several languages, these tide-stemming pamphlets sold for a penny apiece. Two million copies circulated in just one year. The intent was to teach the poor to rely on the virtues of sobriety, industry, humility; to trust in God and the kindness of the gentry; and to revere the British constitution. Amazingly, over one hundred of these morality tales sprang forth in that time—most penned by Hannah More. Sarah and Martha More and Henry Thornton also contributed a few narratives.

In her memoir, Hannah reflected that for many years she had given away annually nearly two hundred Bibles, Common Prayer books, and testaments. To teach the poor to read without providing them with safe books seemed improper. This overarching thought powerfully motivated her in the laborious undertaking of the *Cheap Repository Tracts*. Hannah's words took flight, winging her creativity throughout the apprehensive countryside. Her stories worked to calm a disquieted nation.

Other titles served to reinforce the belief that if one worked hard and stayed sober, blessings would surely result. *The Gin Shop*, subtitled *A Peep into a Prison*, reasoned that "the deadliest pest" in England was not war but drink. Gin was the crack of the eighteenth century. A chemist mixed alcohol, water, and juniper berries, and the poor had the first hard liquor that they could afford. Earlier, the only hard liquors available in England had been expensive brandies. The novelist Henry Fielding wrote that customers left their traditional beer and ale to "get drunk for a penny and dead drunk for two pence." It was in the frightening context of the "gin craze" that London learned the terrors of mass drunkenness. Fielding advocated the prohibition of gin, but the craze only started to subside after gin was taxed at high rates. Thankfully, tea gradually began to rival gin in popularity among both the rich and poor.

After *Village Politics*, More's next political writing came as an indignant reply to the widely publicized atheistic speech that Mr. Jacob Dupont

Frontispiece of *Response on the Speech of M. Dupont.*
Both Hannah More and Edmund Burke agreed that at the
"dark heart of the French Revolution lay an assault on
religion that went far deeper than any attack on kings"
(Stott, 148). Hannah's early tract writing must be seen as
lodged squarely in the context of the French Revolution.

(1735–1813) gave to the National Convention in Paris in December 14,
1792. Mr. Dupont, a member of the French Convention, asserted that religion had no place in public schools—a direct salvo against what Hannah and the anti-Jacobins held dear. In her *Response on the Speech of M.
DuPont,* she argued: "Christians! It is not a small thing—*it is your life.* The
pestilence of irreligion, which you detest, will insinuate itself impercep-
tibly [on yourselves] . . . Let France choose this day whom she will serve;
but, *as for us and our houses, we will serve the Lord.*"

Readers knew the hefty price of two shillings six pence for this piece
(about $8—much more than the half-penny cost of the *Cheap Repository
Tracts)* would go to the French clergy who had escaped to the Isle of Jersey and the English mainland and who now lived in poverty. A couple of
weeks later, *Response to M. DuPont* went into a second edition and soon
had collected £240—the equivalent of about $34,000 in today's value.
Despite Hannah's dislike of loose French habits in general (a character-
istic eighteenth-century ill attitude toward the French), the More sisters
later actually housed French Roman Catholic clergy émigrés at their Barley Wood home. Moreover, they prayed for and with the French, which
was scandalous behavior to many. As a girl, Hannah had learned French
from her older sister, Mary. She later perfected it with the help of cap-
tured French officers in Bristol, who, being officers, "enjoyed the liberty of
parole" in the English port city (Hopkins, 15).

Perhaps Hannah's most popular tract was *The Shepherd of Salisbury Plain*. The hero, a model of piety and hard work, was based on an actual person who raised sixteen children on a meager income. Despite being an embellished, optimistic tale, it remained in print for nearly one hundred years. At the end of the story, the shepherd and his family are lifted from poverty, live in a new and better cottage, and burst into tears of gratitude. The moral is easy to grasp: all things do work together for good to those who love God.

Many think the most famous of the tracts, *The Shepherd of Salisbury Plain,* was Hannah More's masterpiece. "A poor man like me," says the Shepherd, "is seldom called out to do great things, so that it is not by a few great deeds his character can be judged by his neighbors, but by the little round of daily customs he allows himself."

Anne Stott ably summarizes *The History of Hester Brown; or, The New Gown:*

> For a year Hester has been saving up the money she earns from her spinning so that she can have a new gown for the May Day feast. However, her feckless father has been drinking at the alehouse and runs up a gambling debt. As a dutiful daughter, Hester lends him the money she has saved. She resolves to go to the feast in an old dress although she knows she must endure the scornful looks of the other girls. Sure enough, the most industrious girl in town shows

up at the feast in a tawdry gown. Hester survives the humiliation and shortly after, both her parents are converted. She experienced a girl's ultimate horror experience, but due to her generosity to her father, she will eventually move up the social ladder. She will be given the post of under-teacher in the school, on track to being head mistress. More's resolute female characters tackled the tough social problems of the day and showed how virtue was favorably rewarded. (Stott, 188)

Still another tract, *The Riot, or Half a Loaf is Better than No Bread,* came out in 1795 after a poor harvest the previous year. Hooligans had begun attacks on mills and bakers' shops. The laborers believed these merchants hoarded flour to raise prices. Once again, William Wilberforce joined with other philanthropists to quell the discontent of the suffering poor. In 1796, they set up the Society for Bettering the Condition and Increasing the Comforts of the Poor. They distributed pamphlets that contained plans for soup kitchens and subsidized village shops. Some argued that soup kitchens only increased the dependency of the poor. Nevertheless, Hannah and her friends with a moral conscience stepped in to relieve the misery of the underprivileged. This dovetailed with the moral ideology of the *Cheap Repository Tracts:* the wealthy gentry were indeed shouldering their responsibility to help the humble, working poor.

We can say with confidence that neither Hannah's schools nor the *Cheap Repository Tracts* would have been possible without the financial and moral support of her evangelical friends, many of whom lived near and around Clapham Common, referred to earlier as the Clapham Sect. According to *The Christian Observer,* the tracts were "among the mighty barriers that, under God, checked the growth of infidelity and anarchy in Britain" (12:390, 1813).

The *Cheap Repository* stopped printing in 1798, but Hannah's tracts paved the way for the founding of the Religious Tract Society in 1799. A few years later, in 1804, when a Baptist minister suggested the translation of the Bible into Welsh, the British and Foreign Bible Society was founded. This ecumenical stewpot bubbled over with Lutherans, Baptists, Anglicans, dissenters, and evangelicals with the sole purpose of distributing the one text they could all agree upon: the Bible. Henry Thornton served as treasurer. Lord Teignmouth, a former governor-general of India, became its president. The Bible Society played an important role in the energetic evangelical culture of the nineteenth century and beyond. Hannah was proud to play an active role in its founding.

The seeds Hannah More and her philanthropic friends sowed did not fall on stony ground. Her work found later expression in cooperative movements and in the principle of universal literacy. Combatting ignorance, prejudice, bigotry, and attempts to slander her reputation, this talented woman of non-aristocratic roots must be acknowledged as one of the most influential women of her day. Moreover, the popular *Cheap Repository Tracts* demonstrated the "appeal of the mass market" to later publishers and aided the working class's determination to learn to read (Feather, 110).

CHAPTER 11

CŒLEBS, JANE AUSTEN, AND HANNAH MORE

*"Mrs. Montagu and I used always to agree that
you had more wit in your serious writings than other
people had when they meant to be witty."*

—Sir William W. Pepys in a letter
to Hannah More, January 7, 1825

Against the odds for a single woman of non-aristocratic origin, Hannah enjoyed extraordinary success in several careers. A much-praised dramatist and poet as well as a talented member of the Bluestocking and Johnsonian circles, she was now a novelist with a mission. No one worked harder to elevate people's morals at all levels of society. As Mitzi Myers praised her in "Hannah More's Tracts for the Times" (*Fettered or Free*, 266), "This new woman would educate the young and illiterate, succor the unfortunate, amend the debased popular culture of the lower orders, reorient worldly men of every class, and set the national household in order."

Despite her many illnesses, Hannah soldiered on to write her only novel, *Cœlebs in Search of a Wife*. At first issued anonymously and presented in two volumes in 1808, the book stirred almost universal attention. Readers first wondered how to pronounce the hero's name—and then tried to guess the author's identity (*See-lebs* is this author's preferred pronunciation). More's biographer, Anne Stott, suggests "Cœlebs" to be a variation of *celibate*. Charles was the real name of the twenty-three-year-old character, a young man who travels to London and Hampshire to find a wife.

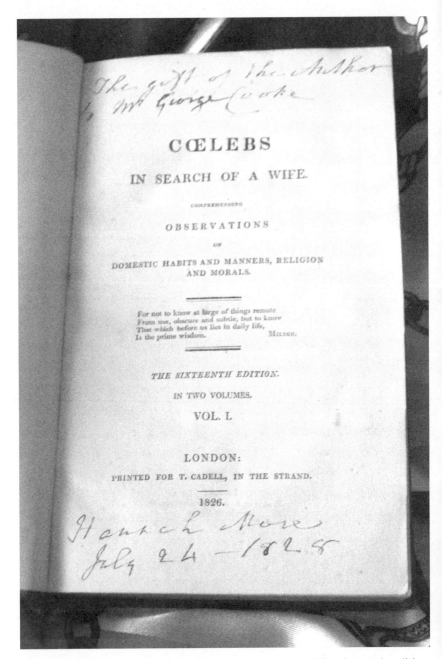

Hannah More's signature in *Cœlebs in Search of a Wife,* sixteenth edition (1826), two volumes. (Photo courtesy of Lori Loftin.)

People quickly guessed Hannah's identity. Now sixty-three years old and famous, she had a reputation as a moral and social revolutionary. By the third edition of *Cœlebs in Search of a Wife*, Hannah More's name was inscribed on the cover of this best-selling novel. People remembered her earlier work with the *Cheap Repository Tracts* and her efforts with William Wilberforce leading up to the Abolition of the Slave Trade Act of 1807 and looked forward to a good read.

Jane Austen (1775–1817), who today is much more famous than Hannah More, also read the novel (everyone, it seemed, was reading *Cœlebs*), but she was dismissive of it. In a letter to her sister, Cassandra, Jane revealed that she did not like evangelicals and mistakenly thought the young man was "Caleb." However, many commentators have noticed a resemblance between Hannah's novel and *Mansfield Park* in Austen's condemnation of the slave trade and the regret over the lack of female educational opportunities. Both novels were didactic.[11] Although More was more explicit about sin, Austen, the daughter of an English clergyman, also wrote about moral failings through her characters, especially pride and greed.

Both Austen and More wrote on similar themes, yet More limited herself to just one novel. Ironically, Austen's novels describe at unending length women looking for husbands to provide social and economic security, while More takes the side of a man seeking a suitable wife of exemplary character. Both More and Austen were opponents of excessive *sensibility*, that shallow notion apparent in many nineteenth-century novels showing women vulnerable to weeping, fainting, or being emotionally weak. To

---

11 Didactic writing, or writing in the "didactic tradition," is often viewed pejoratively by many contemporary critics. Throughout history, many (perhaps most) imaginative and satirical works have contained a moral or political belief of the author. To the modern reader, however, few words used in describing a novel carry more negative connotations than *didactic*. To suggest moral (or immoral) behavior through a character in a novel should not be considered unfavorable propaganda. Austen's didactic methods and intentions are unnoticed today, "sometimes even resented" (Fergus, 10).

A contemporary of Hannah More, Jane Austen earned her place in English literature for her many popular novels. Like Hannah, she was educated primarily by her father as well as through her own reading, but she did not receive in her lifetime the same popularity as the much longer-lived Mrs. More. However, by the second half of the twentieth century, Austen scholarship proliferated, and an enthusiastic Jane Austen fan culture emerged. Austen, like Hannah, was heir to the long tradition of women writing didactically. Central to her writings was the revealing of the shortcomings of female education. Austen's heroines stood proudly as women who could rise above frivolity and be considered sane and balanced creatures. (Sketch of Jane Austen drawn by her sister, Cassandra. Image courtesy of the National Portrait Gallery.)

many at that time, this demonstration of ultrasensitivity with emotional histrionics was considered a virtue.

Jane received no reviews when her first novel *Sense and Sensibility* was published in 1809, but Hannah became inundated with them. Most were good. Many were cool. Some thought *Cœlebs* too stodgy and pretentious and Lucilla, the woman Charles eventually married, too good to be true. What stung Hannah the most was the criticism in the *Christian Observer,* the "house journal" of the Clapham Group. The unsigned reviewer found *Cœlebs* "vulgar."

"Vulgar" in that time usually meant "common," but in spite of that, it still retains a pejorative meaning. What he meant, the reviewer did not specify. It seemed like a cheap shot. A reader today might search the novel in vain for any offending passage. Was Charles's normal sexual response to a pretty young woman the issue that offended the anonymous reviewer? Hannah was apparently less prudish than were her more religious, pietistic friends at the *Christian Observer.* She wanted to challenge the reviewer of the offending passage but let the negative criticism pass uncontested.

Still, Hannah remained deeply wounded by this one particular reviewer, and the authorship remains unknown. Perhaps the negative review led her to conclude the anonymous comment to be an admonition. She did not write another novel. Instead, she took solace in the widespread popularity of the book; it had made £2,000 the first year—far above the £350 Austen made from *Mansfield Park*. *Cœlebs* went into "ten large editions" in the first six months; four American editions quickly followed. Many young women had fallen in love with Charles, her main character. Within ten years, *Cœlebs in Search of a Wife* was translated into German and French. According to Anne Stott, Hannah's only novel became a cultural reference point, a book talked about even when not read (Stott, 277–282).

Those who disliked evangelicals tended to see "methodistic" overtones in *Cœlebs*. What they meant by that also is not clear. However, critics often used the label "Methodist" to deride anything the Wesley brothers promoted, such as extemporaneous prayers and steadfastness in regular meetings, Bible study, and prayers.

Like Hannah More, Jane Austen wrote romantic fiction with social commentary and biting irony. Neither Austen nor More attacked the male authority and prerogatives under which they both lived. Thus, they both tacitly underscored approval of the established hierarchy in England and the church. The paternalism and clerical hierarchy they permitted came from the ethos of their times. Both yearned for a higher status for women within that hierarchy. Both women remained unmarried, and neither was highborn. Both Austen and More were products of their culture and found the social order acceptable, but *only* when those at the top of the social pyramid fulfilled their moral responsibilities. That developing trend toward the emancipation of women would emerge to a measured degree over one hundred years later, culminating in such unprecedented events as women's suffrage and further civil rights for women.

Both authors were women of their times, encountering discrimination based on sex, class, religion, and age. Both could be dubbed "proto-feminists," a term now given to women who, like butterflies, began earlier than most slowly to break out of their constricting chrysalises. As Jane Spencer states in *The Rise of the Woman Novelist* (1986), many today have a "tendency to amnesia" about women's achievements, especially those not from wealthy families. Hannah More is an illustrious case in point. In her study of the art of moral persuasion, Christine Colón points out that "More creates a place for herself by assuming the role of a prophet empowered by God to speak against power structures that did not conform to her evangelical principles" (Colón, 193).

Colón further expands on the rich tradition of Christian women writers to insist on including those overlooked and ignored in the anthologies taught in modern university English literature courses. Christian women writers, contrary to the supposed "constraints of Christianity," found in religion the moral foundation from which to speak out against the evils of their cultures. In current scholarship, Colón asserts, "we have moved

This highly readable edition of *Cœlebs in Search of a Wife,* issued by Broadview Press of Peterborough, Ontario, Canada (2007), contains a helpful introduction and explanatory notes by Patricia Demers. Ms. Demers is Professor of English at the University of Alberta, specializing in women's writing and early modern literature. The cover, *Courtship,* is from the Weldon China Collection, University of King's College, Halifax, Nova Scotia.

far beyond a tradition in English Literature that, at one time, included only Jane Austen, Charlotte and Emily Brontë, George Eliot, and Virginia Woolf." Colón argues for the need to expand the canon even further to include writers from a more explicitly Christian perspective "to capture even more the richness that makes up the ever-expanding world of women writers" (Colón, 195). Hannah contributed part of her considerable earnings to Clergy Daughters' Schools (which the Brontë daughters attended), infirmaries, poorhouses, and missions at home and abroad. In addition, she contended that philanthropy was a woman's profession, and she set a good example.

The evangelical world at that time was deeply suspicious of most plays, dances, and novels, yet Hannah's novel served as a way of propagating the evangelical message.

After the death of David Garrick, and under the influence of certain members of the Clapham Group, Hannah came to renounce the theater and took a negative attitude toward most novels. Reading novels, playing cards, and attending dances she now considered a waste of time. Her Clapham friends thought one's life might be better spent in cultivating the art of serious conversation, letter writing, and reading literature that improved one's virtue. Nevertheless, Hannah used *Cœlebs* to advance her views on women's education and imbue Christian principles to her audience—an instructive technique she had pioneered with her *Cheap Repository Tracts* and *Sacred Dramas*.

To understand this aversion to the theater, fiction, and social dancing, one must look back to Britain's Puritan history and other agents of moral reform. The Puritans shut down the playhouses in 1642. Theaters remained dark until the monarchy was restored in 1660. Dramatic productions were considered "fabrications" and thus a form of sinful entertainment; pleasure for pleasure's sake would lead only to selfish indulgence and dissipation. This sentiment was perpetuated in America by Timothy Dwight (1752–1817), eighth president of Yale University. In his "Essay on the Stage" (1812), he condemned the theater by stating, "A taste for play-going means nothing more or less than the loss of that most valuable treasure, the immortal soul." Jonathan Blanchard (1811–1892), first president of Wheaton College (Illinois), considered novels well-told lies.

The underlying objection to the novel—the whole idea of reading fiction—was that the story was not "true." Happily, the modern evangelical can find in fiction realities that may serve to improve the reader's moral and intellectual development—a pleasant irony when looking back at evangelical history. Many well-told stories offer insightful truths about life and the human condition, and often they can break the frozen sea of one's heart.

CHAPTER 12

Teaching a Nation How to Behave: Hannah More's Didactic Writings

"Luxury! More perilous to youth than storms or quicksand, poverty or chains."

After Hannah More's move to Cowslip Green and taking up her important role of working among the poor, she also strove to maintain her connections in polite society. She produced a number of conduct books for that "polite" society. First, in *Thoughts on the Importance of the Manners of the Great to General Society* (1788), mentioned in chapter 7, she contended that national public morality would remain scandalous until a true reformation of morality transformed the rich and powerful. Good manners and etiquette were a good start, but Hannah wanted people to take the Ten Commandments to heart.

An Estimate of the Religion of the Fashionable World followed in 1790. She published both works anonymously, fearing that if her authorship became known, doors would be shut in her face, and she would find herself in early retirement. The opposite proved to be true. Her literary friends recognized her style and enjoyed the game of pretending to guess the work's authorship. These books sold out immediately and went into multiple editions. One cannot help but think of the Tolkien Middle-earth publishing phenomenon in our current era.

An Estimate of the Religion of the Fashionable World took up the decline of Christianity, the neglect of religious education (which she had witnessed firsthand when she set up her schools in the West Country), and the lack of morals without a religious foundation. Later she rejoiced to learn that, after reading her books, Queen Charlotte (George III's wife) stopped summoning an outside hairdresser on the Sabbath and used instead an attendant already on duty (Hopkins, 223).

Hannah described three religious classes in England. One class, she observed, consisted of pious Christians who gave evidence in their lives of "the peace of God which passeth all understanding" but were unable to give a reason for the hope that was in them. Another group contained the nominal "Christians" who believed themselves Christians only because they were born in a Christian country. The third class was composed of "actual waverers" who were influenced by "the English infidels," such as David Hume (1711–1776) and Edward Gibbon (1737–1794), and the French atheists (Thompson, 147–148). More intended to shake loose the religious complacency of the rich and respectable—those in group two. Her new evangelical fervor motivated her to preach to the aristocratic up-and-outs as well as to the down-and-outs.

Three additional works focusing on education flowed from her impassioned pen. They stirred up considerable debate due to Hannah More's view of women and their role in society. In 1799, she published *Strictures in the Modern System of Female Education with a View to the Principles and Conduct of Women of Rank and Fortune.* (Books with long, descriptive titles were normative in Hannah's day.) It went through thirteen editions and sold more than nineteen thousand copies. *Strictures,* a large, two-volume work, was mainly a response to Mary Wollstonecraft's *Vindication of the Rights of Women,* published in 1792.

Next came *Hints Towards Forming the Character of a Princess* (1805). Designed as a course of study for Princess Charlotte, daughter of the Prince of Wales, who might become the queen of England, *Hints* offered a select curriculum for a high-class education.

Mary Wollstonecraft (1759–97). Mary Wollstonecraft was born in London in 1759 and was self-educated, as were many women of her day. She is best known for her book *A Vindication of the Rights of Women,* in which she refuted the opinion among men that women were morally, emotionally, and mentally inferior to them. She moved to France for a while, becoming friends with Thomas Paine and other revolutionaries. There, she wrote many essays and a history of the French Revolution. She also bore a daughter, Fanny, in 1794. Mary began calling herself Mrs. Imlay to bestow legitimacy upon her child by Gilbert Imlay (1754–1828), but he never married her. Mary's unorthodox lifestyle destroyed her reputation in her lifetime, but today she is best known as a founding feminist philosopher. In 1797, she married the British political reformer and philosopher William Godwin (1765–1836) after becoming pregnant with his child. At age thirty-eight, Mary died from septicemia after giving birth to her second daughter, Mary Wollstonecraft Godwin. This daughter later changed her name to Mary Shelley upon her marriage to Percy Bysshe Shelley, Lord Byron. She is best known for her horror novel, *Frankenstein* (1818).

Hannah undertook *Hints Towards Forming the Character of a Young Princess* at the request of the Bishop of Bristol, the Right Reverend Robert Gray (1762–1835). The bishop urged Hannah to design a reading curriculum suitable for the education of Princess Charlotte, then only nine years old. What continued to be truly remarkable about Hannah's literary output and influence were the many prominent men in her life who admired her adept writing skills. If they wanted something expressed well, they not only trusted her but begged her to put *their* thoughts into writing.

Princess Charlotte, named after her grandmother, was the only legitimate child of the Prince of Wales, later George IV. Her grandfather had been George III, the "mad king" who was on the throne during the American War for Independence. Her education became a matter of great concern on the part of those who knew about her troubled upbringing. Her parents quarreled and lived separately most of Charlotte's life. Her father was rowdy, piled up debts, and quarreled with his father the king. He was not considered a suitable parent for the woman who was in line to be queen of England. Charlotte's mother, Princess Caroline of Brunswick, was also a person of dubious conduct and the center of various scandals. The bishop in charge of Charlotte's religious instruction knew of the mother's sometimes wild behaviors. He became concerned that she was not receiving proper instruction from her ladies in waiting; this motivated him to seek help from Hannah More.

After Hannah's book was published, the bishop read to Charlotte from it, but the unbookish princess often grew bored. We do not know if she ever read the recommended books on English and ancient history, Plutarch, Fénelon, or the Bible. Nevertheless, Hannah wanted Charlotte to be a positive force for good. In the book, Hannah highlighted Mary II (1662-1694) and her marriage to William of Orange (1650–1702)—*both* "appointed by Providence to protect our liberties." William and Mary ruled jointly "by the Grace of God, King and Queen of England, France, and Ireland, Defenders of the Faith, etc." in the seventeenth century—proof that the monarchy allowed female succession. Hannah would do her utmost to help Charlotte get a good education. *Hints Towards Forming the Character of a Young Princess* never sold as well as the other conduct books, but the person who mattered most—the girl who would be queen—heard it read.

Wedding engraving of Princess Charlotte and Prince Leopold of Saxe-Coburg-Saalfeld (later king of the Belgians). Following a year and a half of happy marriage, Charlotte died on November 6, 1817, at age twenty-one, after giving birth to a stillborn son. Charlotte had begun her pregnancy as a healthy and robust young woman, but after months of bloodletting and a strict diet, an accepted medical practice prescribed by her physician, she grew frail and weak. Five hours after her delivery, she died from postpartum hemorrhage. Her physician, unable to live with the criticism and knowledge that he was responsible for the two royal deaths, committed suicide three months later. Following this triple tragedy, a new "rational intervention" in obstetrics came to the fore. Ergot (ergotamine developed from rye plants to stimulate uterine contractions), forceps, and anesthesia were introduced to make birth safer and less painful.

In her sixties, Hannah still travelled to London for at least two months of the year, dividing her time between her friends—Mrs. Garrick, Bishop Porteus, Lord Teignmouth, and one or two others. The schools still occupied the best part of her time, and her frequent illnesses interfered with her writing. During the London visit in 1798, she encountered Sir William Weller Pepys (1741–1825), master of the Chancery Court and a friend from the Bluestocking circle. (In England at that time, the judge, or master, in this court worked specifically for the king in resolving many land disputes.) She consulted Pepys about her plans for *Strictures*. He wrote to encourage her, noting that her influence in the sphere of women's education was more extensive than she could imagine. She took his advice to heart. In the very beginning of chapter 1, she states her thesis: "Among the talents for the application of which women of the higher class will be particularly accountable, there is one, the importance of which they can scarcely rate too highly. This talent is influence."

Sir William Weller Pepys (1758–1825) was among the men who attended the *Bas Blue* gatherings and proved a favorite with the great and learned ladies. (Other male attendees were Horace Walpole, Samuel Johnson, David Garrick, Benjamin Stillingfleet, and Sir Joshua Reynolds.) On December 1, 1792, he wrote a letter showing his genuine alarm over the events in France: "Both Mrs. Montagu and I most earnestly request you to exert your talents for the good of your country, which is in great peril; do pray set yourself to work directly, and remember that if you should be an instrument to prevent the horrible scenes of confusion and bloodshed, which have laid France desolate, you will have a greater reward than the applause of all the Literati in Europe" (*A Later Pepys,* vol. 2, 219–220).

In *Strictures,* Hannah wrote to call women "to raise the depressed tone of public morals, and to awaken the drowsy spirit of religious principle." She lamented the limits placed on women who had not received adequate education. On the other hand, she warned women not to become "female warriors" or "female politicians," thus spoiling their noble sphere of influence.

More continually urged women to improve their minds, but in the framework of Christian humility. She wanted to be seen as the polar opposite of Mary Wollstonecraft and her atheistic, Jacobinian sentiments. Although this stance made her popular among conservatives, feminists ever since have tended to ignore her considerable contributions to literature and the education of women, especially among the poor.

Ann (Nancy) Hasseltine Judson (1789–1826): At age sixteen in Bradford, Massachusetts, Ann Hasseltine took up reading Hannah More's *Strictures on Female Education* and resolved to "seek a life of usefulness." At twenty-three, she married Adoniram Judson. Soon after the wedding they sailed for Calcutta, a stop on the way to Rangoon. They reached Rangoon five months later. A person of decided character and remarkable courage, Ann Judson is considered the "mother of modern missions." She died of smallpox in 1826 in Burma (Myanmar) in her thirty-seventh year, but not before she had translated several books of the Bible into Burmese.

Despite Hannah's dislike for Wollstonecraft's politics, both women agreed that females had been disadvantaged and held back by a faulty education system. They also agreed that the "cult of sensibility" had trivialized women, unwittingly making them slaves to their "fragile" emotions. Despite More's warning about women aspiring to become female politicians (legally impossible at that time), she urged the keepers of hearth and home to be loyal and moral guardians of their country and to keep abreast of strategic public issues.

In setting herself up as the opposite of Wollstonecraft, Hannah has unfortunately—and frequently—been considered by historians to be an antifeminist. However, in taking her life and works as a whole, Hannah should be

Practical Piety;

OR,

THE INFLUENCE OF THE RELIGION OF
THE HEART

ON THE

CONDUCT OF THE LIFE.

BY HANNAH MORE.

The fear of God begins with the heart, and purifies and rectifies it; and from the heart, thus rectified, grows a conformity in the life, the words, and the actions.—*Sir Matthew Hale's Contemplations.*

AMERICAN SUNDAY-SCHOOL UNION:
1816 CHESTNUT STREET, PHILADELPHIA.

Although undated, this edition of *Practical Piety* gives but one example of the international scope and dissemination of Hannah More's writings. The American Sunday School Union, 1816 Chestnut Street, Philadelphia, began publishing some of her work in 1824. (Image courtesy of the Castle House Museum)

seen as a proto-feminist—a word unknown in her day. (In our modern era of feminist studies, a proto-feminist is an individual who laid the groundwork for the feminists who followed, both biblical and secular. These early mold-breakers often encountered strident backlash from those needing to confine women to fixed roles.) More, like Wollstonecraft, believed women had been shortchanged by their negligible education. Almost as a continuation of her *Estimate of the Religion of the Fashionable World,* Hannah reiterated her beliefs that women especially, armed with transformative evangelical beliefs, were the true architects of a good and just society.

Practical Piety, a deeply spiritual book published in 1811, soon ran to ten editions. Hannah wrote in chapter 2, "No man ought to flatter himself that he is in the favour of God, whose life is not consecrated to the service of God." In a final chapter, "Happy Deaths," she was perhaps looking forward to her own passing when she wrote, "There is no *happy death* but that which conducts to a *happy immortality;* no joy in putting off the body, if we have not put on the Lord Jesus Christ."

Next came *Christian Morals* (1812), and at age sixty-nine, Hannah wrote *Essay on the Character and Writings of St. Paul* in two volumes, also well received. In 1819, at age seventy-four, she published *Moral Sketches of Prevailing Opinions and Manners, Foreign and Domestic, with Reflections on Prayer.* This work was directed chiefly against those who followed the rage for copying French manners, customs, and loose morals. When it came to using her considerable influence, Hannah More just could not stop writing for the causes she believed in.

Hannah More in her later years. At age eighty-two, Hannah collected from her later works and published *The Spirit of Prayer* (1825)—her last literary effort. She commented once to a friend that the only remarkable thing belonging to her as an author was that she had written eleven volumes after the age of sixty. Eleven volumes after the age of sixty surely ranks her work as a remarkable output for anyone.

John Scandrett Harford (1785–1866), a staunch Quaker and abolitionist, was also a friend of William Wilberforce. John and his brothers donated the grounds to St David's College, Lampeter, in 1820, now part of the University of Wales.

CHAPTER 13

The Tumultuous Final Years

"Do not indulge romantic ideas of superhuman excellence.
Remember that the fairest creature is a fallen creature."

In Hannah's late years, sorrow struck. Between 1813 and 1819, her four sisters died. The last to go was Martha (Patty), Hannah's trusty lieutenant in all her benevolent schemes. They had occupied themselves with their schools and the planning and providing for the annual school feasts. In addition, they had also started a Wrington branch of the British and Foreign Bible Society.

Hannah More not only lost her sisters but also keenly mourned the national tragedy of the death of Princess Charlotte (1817). Hannah had hoped that this young queen would lead the nation down a more righteous path. The deaths of her other friends—Mrs. Garrick in 1822, Joshua and Frances Reynolds, Mrs. Montagu, Horace Walpole, William Pepys, Henry Thornton—all reminded her of her own mortality. She wrote to Wilberforce in 1827 that none of her contemporaries remained.

Always generous and outgoing, Mrs. More began to make new friends. The earliest was her neighbor, John Scandrett Harford, the son of a prominent banker in Bristol who would inherit Blaise Castle in Bristol. John rallied around Mrs. More in her old age when she was obliged to leave Barley Wood because of deceitful domestic help.

John Scandrett Harford's sizeable estate, Blaise House and Castle, is now owned by the city of Bristol and open to the public.

With her sisters gone, Hannah found her health diminishing. She spent most of her days in her room and in prayer. Visitors came to the upstairs sitting room. She enjoyed showing them mementos from her support of foreign missionary societies. Due to her generosity, she unwittingly let people take advantage of her, especially her servants, who diverted money that she thought was being taken to charities. Without her consent, they held parties in the coach house where intoxication was frequent.

At first, Hannah refused to hear of their misdeeds, because she had hoped to end her years in her beloved Barley Wood. Nevertheless, her good friend Dr. Whalley, who had been one of her champions during the Blagdon Controversy, and John Scandrett Harford, her wealthy neighbor, knew she was too old to grapple with all the domestic disloyalty. They secretly arranged for her to move to Windsor Terrace, Clifton by the Sea. There she would be near friends who could look in on her. The dishonest servants did not know of her sudden departure until the day John had her whisked away in his own carriage. She took one final, thoughtful look at her gardens, saying, "I am driven like Eve out of Paradise, but not like Eve, by angels" (an allusion to John Milton's *Paradise Lost)*. The servants were quickly removed from the premises so they could not do further damage and were given three months' wages instead of notice. Her own beloved carriage horses were sold.[12]

---

12 Patricia Demers in *The World of Hannah More* states that William Henry Harford, a younger brother of John Scandrett Harford, bought the estate

Her residence at 4 Windsor Terrace had a view over the Avon Gorge, not far from Bristol, where her life had begun. Her doctor lived nearby. Although saddened by having to move at age eighty-two from her beloved Barley Wood, she carried to her new elegant house the same cheerful and contented mind that had distinguished her through life. Her friends crowded around her in an effort to express their continued attachment. Lady Olivia Sparrow and the Roberts sisters, Mary and Margaret, were of great comfort to Hannah during the last five years of her life. (Margaret's brother, William, had access through Margaret to More's correspondence after she died. His *Memoirs of the Life and Correspondence of Mrs. Hannah More* appeared in 1834, soon after her death.)

In a letter to Wilberforce six months after her move in 1828, Hannah wrote, "I cannot express the joy your most welcome letter gave me . . . I am diminishing my worldly cares. I have greatly lessened my household expenses, which enables me to maintain my schools, and to enlarge my charities . . . My removal hence has been providentially directed for my good. I have two pious clergymen near me, whom I call my chaplains . . . My most kind and skillful physician, Dr. Carrick, who used to have twelve miles to come to me, has now not much above two hundred yards . . . By the Blessing of God on his skills, I am nearly recovered, but have still to feed chiefly on drugs" (Taylor, 405).

William Wilberforce continued his campaign for the complete abolition of slavery, but due to poor health, he resigned from Parliament in 1826.

---

in a private sale. (John was the touted model for "Charles" in More's novel *Cœlebs in Search of a Wife*.) The Harfords occupied Barley Wood—with a few minor changes—for most of the nineteenth century. Henry Herbert Will, of the tobacco empire, bought the house in 1897. It stayed in the Will family for seventy years. In 1974, a consortium of building companies, the H.A.T. Group Limited, bought and occupied Barley Wood as their administrative headquarters. In 1978, the Locke and Porteus urns were reerected on the porch outside the group chairman's office. In 1990, Barley Wood housed a drug treatment center that closed in 2008. On eleven acres, Frank Knight offered it for sale in 2012 for £1,650,00.

4 Windsor Terrace, the new four-story building situated on high ground in the new elegant suburb of Clifton, enjoyed a view overlooking the Avon River gorge in one direction and the city of Bristol in the other. Hannah More lived here the last five years of her life. A historic preservation plaque to the left of the door reads "Hannah More (1745–1833), Authoress, lived here 1828–1833." The residence remains privately owned and in good repair.

His efforts led to the Slavery Abolition Act of 1833, which abolished slavery in most of the British Empire. He died on July 29, 1833, just three days after hearing the news that Parliament had passed the act. It is doubtful that his dear friend, Hannah, was aware either of his passing or of his funeral in Westminster Abbey, where he was buried next to his friend William Pitt. The two evangelical Christians, More and Wilberforce, who together had worked with Thomas Clarkson, Granville Sharp, Charles Middleton, and others for twenty-six years against the British slave trade, died the same year. Mrs. More was in her eighty-ninth year, Wilberforce in his seventy-fourth.

Hannah More kept her wits about her until the last few months of her life. She followed the political world with much interest and continued her correspondence with her many friends, especially Marianne Thornton, in whose children she delighted. However, toward the end of her life, Mrs. More's friends noticed a few symptoms of mental deterioration. Her memory became impaired. By the fall of 1832, she developed pneumonia-like symptoms with fevers that wasted her strength. She lingered in bed for another year, but in the early morning of September 7, 1833, her gentle breathing stopped.

On the thirteenth of September, her remains were brought to the family vault at Wrington where her sisters had been buried. She had wished that her funeral be private, but many wanted to pay tribute to this benevolent woman on her journey to interment. As the mournful procession passed through Bristol, all the shops closed, and the church bells tolled. As her body arrived in Wrington, many of the neighboring clergy, gentry, and laborers, accompanied by schoolchildren, lined the pathway. It seemed an appropriate tribute to have the poor mingling with the great and titled. The Reverend Thomas Tregenna Biddulph, rector of St. James, Bristol—the Mores' church for many, many years—conducted the services.

The following Sunday, the Reverend Henry Thompson, M.A., curate of Wrington, Somerset, preached a sermon on Acts 9:36: "This woman was full of good works and almsdeeds." The sermon was later published in the "Christian Remembrances" for the month of October, 1833, by E. Clay, Printer, Bread-Street- Hill, London; a copy of the same may be found in the Rare Book Room, Cambridge University Library. The Reverend Henry Thompson also wrote *The Life of Hannah More with Notices of her Sisters*, published in 1848 by T. Cadell, Strand, London. In those days it was not uncommon for a minister to preach a sermon of tribute eulogizing the life and memory of someone recently deceased.

By their industry, Hannah and her sisters had accumulated a handsome income to provide for others. From her writings alone, Hannah had earned £30,000, a remarkable achievement for a nonaristocratic, single woman in the eighteenth century. Her fortune was distributed among some seventy religious societies and charitable projects. In her will, she remembered well over one hundred friends, many in small bequests. Nineteen guineas was a favorite sum, as there was no tax on bequests under twenty pounds.

Considering her many physical ailments, Hannah More's persistence in adversity made her accomplishments all the more remarkable. Her friends remarked that when she was laid aside by an illness, they expected a new book from her. Mrs. More's last literary effort came at age eighty-two in 1825. She had collected her earlier writings and had them published in a little volume with a short preface entitled *The Spirit of Prayer*. The figure that emerges in those last full years is a woman who met the challenges of

A Christmas illustration from *Cheap Repository Tracts.* Hannah More also contributed a few hymns to her anthology of poems. A favorite is her Christmas hymn, which can be sung to the tune of "Love Divine All Loves Excelling" (Beecher) or "Joyful, Joyful, We Adore Thee" (Hymn to Joy).

A New Christmas Hymn

O How wondrous is the story
Of our blest Redeemer's birth!
See the mighty Lord of Glory
Leaves his heaven to visit earth!

Hear with transport, every creature,
Hear the gospel's joyful sound:
Christ appears in human nature,
In our sinful world is found!

None but he who did create us,
Could redeem from sin and hell;
None but he could reinstate us
In the rank from which we fell.

'Twas to bring us endless pleasure,
He our suffering nature bore;
'Twas to give us heavenly treasure
He was willing to be poor.

Come, ye poor, some comfort gather,
Faint not in the race you run;
Hard the lot your gracious Father
Gave his dear, his only Son.

See your Savior now ascended;
See, he looks with pity down:
Trust him, all will soon be mended;
Bear his cross, you'll share his crown.

GRAVE OF MRS. HANNAH MORE, WRINGTON CHURCHYARD.

Between a yew and a willow, a plain stone marks the spot where "the five good sisters sleep together in Christ." (Sketch by H. Thompson.) It is headed: "Beneath are Deposited the Mortal Remains of Five Sisters." Then follow their names and the dates of their deaths:

Mary More	Died 18th of April 1813	Aged 75 years
Elizabeth More	Died 16th of June 1816	Aged 76 years
Sarah More	Died 17th of May 1817	Aged 74 years
Martha More	Died 16th of Sept 1819	Aged 72 years
Hannah More	Died 7th of Sept 1833	Aged 88 years

All these died in the Faith
Accepted in the Beloved
Hebrews 11: 13   Ephesians 1:6

the great and the lowly with equal courage and hope. She accepted what she felt were her moral responsibilities to act more fearlessly than most women of her time, and she did not shrink back.

A sign near the grave was added to help Hannah More's many visitors decipher the letterings on the moss and lichen-covered tombstone. (Photo courtesy of William Phemister.)

The Wrington Church, 2012, where Hannah More and her sisters are buried. Little has changed since 1833 except for the vibrant congregation that continues to worship on Sundays. They pass her commemorative bust as they enter and leave by the main entrance of the church. (Photo courtesy of William Phemister.)

CHAPTER 14

HANNAH MORE'S LEGACY AND THE NEW WOMEN'S MOVEMENT

"Oh, the joy of young ideas painted on the mind,
in the warm, glowing colors fancy spreads on objects not
yet known, when all is new and all is lovely."

Women writing in the late eighteenth and early nineteenth centuries were well aware of the changes taking place in their world. The evangelical movement promoted awareness that women were moral beings responsible for their own personal relationship to God and their need to become contributing members of society. The Sunday school movement and Hannah More's schools had produced readers among the lower classes. Now it was necessary to provide quality reading material to mentor and mold the receptive minds and hearts of these new readers.

Hannah More believed she had a moral duty not only to shape high society (as in the case of the royal princess Charlotte) but also to provide suitable reading material for the poor. She felt an ongoing obligation to those she helped to educate in the rural towns in the west of England. William Wilberforce and Bishop Porteus, for example, actually enlisted her in their campaigns against slavery. They also feared a revolution against the British monarchy. Both men were keenly aware of what was happening just across the channel in France—first the Revolution, then the Reign

Cheap Repository.

SUNDAY READING.

THE

GENERAL RESURRECTION,

AND

DAY OF JUDGMENT:

Being a Description, taken from S. . . . . , of some of the
Events which will come to pass at the end of the World.

SOLD BY HOWARD AND EVANS,

(Printers to the CHEAP REPOSITORY for Moral and Religious
Tracts) No. 41 and 42 Long-Lane, West-Smithfield,
and J. HATCHARD, 190, Piccadilly, London: by
J. BINNS, Bath:—And by all Booksellers, Newsmen,
and Hawkers, in Town and Country.

₊ Great allowance will be made to Shopkeepers and Hawkers

Price ONE PENNY, Or, Six-shillings, per Hundred.

Entered at Stationers' Hall.

An illustrated cover from one her *Cheap Repository Tracts,* written between 1795–1798. (*Resurrection* was written for a Sunday edition). Writing is an art, but it is also a craft. A master of versatility, Hannah More used a variety of storytelling strategies, different voices, and diverse perspectives. She connected with the aristocrats (her one novel could only be understood by the educated elite), but also with the laboring poor—many of whom she had taught to read in the schools she founded. Hannah More's writings reached the hearts of millions for good, reminding people of their better selves and their duty to God and country.

of Terror, followed by the Napoleonic Wars. They admired and respected Hannah More for her integrity and her artful way with words. They wanted her considerable talents on their side.

Yet, many modern literary critics find Hannah More too hierarchical for their feminist sensibilities. It is much easier to ignore her and focus on Mary Wollstonecraft's more activist and secular role in *The Vindication of the Rights of Women*. However, both More and Wollstonecraft sounded similar themes in taking women seriously, urging better female education, and vigorously correcting the notion that females were not capable of important political and philanthropic endeavors. Her writings were simply a response to the specific moral and social issues of her time.

Hannah clearly reflected the same style that other eighteenth-century fiction writers used to echo the sexist reality of their day. Nevertheless, despite More's critics in the strictly Calvinistic world (as in the tart unsigned review of *Cœlebs* in the *Christian Observer*) who were deeply suspicious of the theater, the novel, and even the idea of reading as entertainment, her one novel gave encouragement to other women writers who propagated the evangelical cause through their writings. Bebbington notes, "In an age when avenues into any sphere outside the home were being closed [to women], Christian zeal brought [her] into prominence. Hannah More's Evangelicalism . . . allied faith, hope, and charity to national purpose" (Bebbington, 26).

Hannah More may have encountered more attacks in her lifetime than other women authors of her day simply because of her celebrity status in the literary and public world. She was one of the first women of her social status to achieve such high visibility, but today, oddly, she is overlooked and even ignored. Her strong neo-Puritan sensibilities do not resonate with modern, secularist culture. Few people outside the realm of literary academics have heard of her.

Hannah More, like Wilberforce, experienced a midlife conversion, strongly influenced by the Methodists and John Newton. She was guilty of encouraging extemporaneous prayers, a practice unknown in her local parish church. Like Wilberforce, she never left her beloved Church of England. Like Wilberforce, she became dedicated to changing England through Christian principles. Both More and Wilberforce believed the key to national reform lay with a morally improved royalty and gentry. They both held that even the healing of class divisions was possible through a newly revitalized Christianity.

One cannot overemphasize the influence of the evangelical revivals of John and Charles Wesley and George Whitefield on the changes in hierarchical assumptions, social class distinctions, and structures of authority in their day. Donald Dayton, in *Discovering an Evangelical Heritage,* points to certain innovative and experimental practices, such as teaching and even preaching, that allowed new roles for women in the church. John Wesley himself, by the end of his life, gave approval to laymen (and a few women) to preach and teach the Bible, acts not permitted by the Church of England. Though not theologically trained, Hannah used her writing talents to express her revitalized Christianity.

By the beginning of the nineteenth century, Bible commentators began to express new conclusions. Dayton quotes commentator Adam Clark: "Under the blessed spirit of Christianity, [women] have equal rights, equal privileges, and equal blessings, and let me add, they are equally useful" (Dayton, 88). Abolitionists like Hannah More, who had overcome the biblical defenses of slavery, now began to see fresh interpretations of the Bible that supported the new women's movement. Galatians 3:28 was a major New Testament text that emphasized, "There is neither Jew nor Greek, there is neither bond nor free, there is neither male nor female: for ye are all one in Christ Jesus." However, Hannah in her lifetime was not able to break away from her own cultural conditioning, despite the leveling force and implications of the feminist awakenings expressed in the Galatians passage.

Hannah did not live long enough to see the results of evangelical revivalism as it spread to America. In 1833, the year she died, Oberlin College was founded in Oberlin, Ohio. It was the first school anywhere in the world dedicated to educating both men and women and people of color. (Bishop Chase's school, Kenyon College in Ohio, only admitted men.) The enlightened first president of Oberlin, Asa Mahan, wanted chiseled onto his tombstone, "The first man, in the history of the race who conducted women, in connection with members of the opposite sex, through a full course of liberal education, and conferred upon her the high degrees which had hitherto been the exclusive prerogatives of men" (Dayton, 157).

Twenty years later in 1853, farther west in a prairie town named Wheaton, a group of pioneering Methodists founded the Illinois Institute for "the higher education of both men and women." It would later be renamed Wheaton College under the leadership of the abolitionist and educator Jonathan Blanchard. Blanchard, who recognized the quick minds of his own daughters, vowed early on that he would never be the president of an institution that would not permit women to learn as well as men. He also commended others who provided such opportunities to women.

Jonathan Blanchard (1811–1892) at about age twenty-five. Motivated by love for God and service to others, Blanchard invested great energy into social reform, especially in crusades against slavery and the Masons. His college was the first institute of higher education in Illinois to graduate both women and blacks. (Image courtesy of Wheaton College Archives.)

It is not surprising then, when looking back through the rearview mirror, that literary critics focus on their own feminist sensibilities and ignore More's very important role in working for the abolition of the slave trade and the education of the poor. Yet, sympathy and respect, not disregard, must be granted to the religiously motivated reformers of influence in the eighteenth century. In the twentieth century, the Reverend

Martin Luther King Jr.'s Christian convictions were the prime influence for his nonviolent work in the civil rights movement. In her century, two hundred years before Martin Luther King Jr., Hannah More championed moral and social revolutionary causes based on her Christian convictions. Her life actively encompassed a complex mixture of social, religious, and cultural innovation, and she was indisputably a "tract writer of genius" (Mitzi Myers in Schofield and Macheski, *Fettered or Free,* 268).

During the first half of her life, Hannah More won success in England as a dramatist, poet, and witty, talented member of the Bluestocking and Johnsonian circles. After her conversion to evangelicalism and the death of David Garrick, she abandoned the theater, despite her fame in London. Instead, as noted in an earlier chapter, she grew weary of the London scene and retreated to her home in Cowslip Green and later to Barley Wood, but she continued to write with conviction.

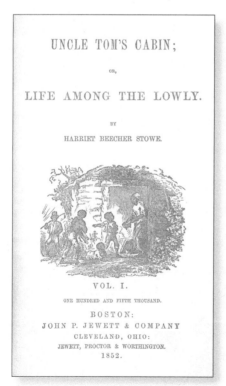

Uncle Tom's Cabin, a vital antislavery tool, was the best-selling novel of the nineteenth century. Following the Bible, it was the second-best-selling book of that century.

	£.	s.	d.
To the Bristol Infirmary	1,000	0	0
,, Anti-Slavery Society	500	0	0
,, London Pious Clergy	500	0	0
,, London Clerical Education Society	100	0	0
,, Moravian Missionary Society	200	0	0
,, Welsh College	400	0	0
,, Bristol Clerical Education Society	100	0	0
,, Hibernian Society	200	0	0
,, Reformation Society	200	0	0
,, Religious Tract Society	150	0	0
,, Irish Scripture Reading Society	150	0	0
,, Burmese Mission	200	0	0
,, Society for the Conversion of the Jews	200	0	0
,, Society for Printing the Scriptures at Serampoore	100	0	0
,, Baptist Missionary Society	100	0	0
,, London Seaman's Bible Society	100	0	0
,, Liverpool Seaman's Bible Society	100	0	0
,, London Missionary Society	100	0	0
,, Society for Printing the Hebrew Scriptures	100	0	0
,, British and Foreign Bible Society	1,000	0	0
,, Church Missionary Society	1,000	0	0
,, Society for Educating Clergymen's Daughters	200	0	0
,, Diocese of Ohio	200	0	0
,, Trustees of the New Church at Mangotsfield	150	0	0
,, Bristol Stranger's Friend Society	100	0	0
,, Bristol Society for the Relief of Small Debtors	100	0	0
,, Bristol Penitentiary	100	0	0
,, Bristol Orphan Society	100	0	0
,, Bristol Philosophical Institution	100	0	0
,, London Stranger's Friend Society	100	0	0
,, Commissioners of Foreign Missions in America, towards the School at Ceylon, called 'Barley Wood'	100	0	0
,, Newfoundland School Society	100	0	0
,, Society for the Distressed Vaudoise	100	0	0
,, Clifton Dispensary	100	0	0
,, Bristol District for Visiting the Poor	100	0	0
,, Irish Society	100	0	0
,, Sailors' Home Society	100	0	0
,, Christian Knowledge Society	50	0	0
,, Bristol Misericordia Society	50	0	0
,, Bristol Samaritan Society	30	0	0
,, Bristol Temple Infant School	50	0	0
,, Prayer-Book and Homily Society	50	0	0
,, London Lock Hospital	50	0	0
,, London Refuge for the Destitute	50	0	0
,, Gaelic School	50	0	0
,, Society for Female Schools in India	50	0	0
,, Keynsham School	50	0	0

	£.	s.	d.
To the Cheddar School	50	0	0
,, For Books for Ohio	50	0	0
,, Bristol and Clifton Female Anti-Slavery Society	50	0	0
,, Clifton Lying-in Charity	50	0	0
,, Clifton Infant School	50	0	0
,, Clifton National School	50	0	0
,, Clifton Female Hibernian Society	50	0	0
,, Temple Poor	50	0	0
,, For Pews in the Temple Church	50	0	0
,, Bristol Harmonica	20	0	0
,, Edinburgh Sabbath Schools	20	0	0
,, Shipham Female Club	50	0	0
,, Cheddar Female Club	20	0	0
,, Poor Printers' Fund	20	0	0
,, For Shipham Poor	50	0	0
,, Minister of Wrington, for distribution among the Poor	20	0	0
,, Minister of Cheddar, for distribution among the Poor	20	0	0
,, Minister of Nailsea, for the Poor	5	0	0
,, The Kildare School Society, Dublin	500	0	0
	£.9,675	0	0

Hannah More's will: Note the many charities she supported at her death. She generously distributed a similar amount during her lifetime.

Hannah More firmly believed that the moral and cultural achievements of Great Britain and the larger world should be based on Judeo-Christian principles. She expounded her views in *Moral Sketches of Prevailing Opinions and Manners, Foreign and Domestic with Reflections on Prayer,* published in 1820. Hannah also supported the expansion of the missionary movement and opened her purse to the Christian Missionary Society and the Society for Promoting Female Education in the East (India); she also funded the Barley Wood School in Ceylon. Many orphan children in Africa were named after her. The passionate involvement of Hannah More and other women like her in the antislavery cause would eventually culminate in Harriet Beecher Stowe's *Uncle Tom's Cabin* (1852).

Hannah More died four years before the eighteen-year-old Victoria was crowned queen of England in 1837. Because Hannah's ideas of religion-based social responsibility resembled those of the enlarging empire under Queen Victoria, biographer Anne Stott dubbed Hannah "the first Victorian." Characteristics of the Victorian era—enterprise, initiative, and the importance of the family—were Hannah More's traits as well. Her personal faith empowered her to speak truth to men in power and to influence many other female Christian writers.

Despite her relative obscurity today, Hannah More embodied much more than a mere footnote to history, as some would have us think. Her enormous contributions to education and philanthropy alone, not to mention her social activism as an abolitionist, and her involvement in pressure group politics are worthy of sustained attention.

As one of her biographers concludes, Hannah More was not the cold stranger of the past. She was a woman who devoted her long career to "galvanizing women in the middle and upper ranks to act, not as domestic ornaments, but as thinking, engaged, and responsible social beings" (Demers, 131). Her story helps us discover that hundreds of years ago, God was calling normal women in trying circumstances to do the extraordinary. Hannah More is inspiring, not because she was perfect, but because she was faithful.

Hannah More Chronology

Adapted from The Victorian Web, Anne Stott,
Open University (UK)

1707   The Act of Union unites England and Wales with Scotland.

1745   Hannah More is born, February 2, at Fishponds, Stapleton,
            Bristol, the fourth of the five daughters of Jacob More, a
            schoolmaster, and Mary (Grace) More, a farmer's daughter.

1758   Her eldest sister, Mary More, opens a girls' boarding school
            in Trinity Street, Bristol.

1763   Britain wins control of France's North American empire as
            a result of the Seven Years' War.

c. 1767   More visits the estate of William Turner at Belmont,
            Somerset, and later accepts his proposal of marriage.

1773   Engagement to Turner is finally broken off. More accepts an
            annuity of £200/year. Bristol printer Sarah Farley publishes
            The Search After Happiness.

1774   More goes to London; on her second visit meets David
            Garrick, Samuel Johnson, Edmund Burke, and Elizabeth
            Montagu; supports Burke's election campaign in Bristol.
            Thomas Cadell publishes *The Inflexible Captive* and becomes
            her main publisher.

1775   The Theatre Royal, Bath, performs *The Inflexible Captive*.

1776   More becomes the Garricks' semi-permanent houseguest at
            the Adelphi (London) and Hampton (Middlesex); witnesses
            Garrick's farewell performances at the Drury Lane Theatre.
            The American War for Independence begins with the
            Declaration of Independence.

1777   Publishes *Essays on Various Subjects,* her first conduct
            book, dedicated to her Bluestocking friend, Elizabeth
            Montagu.

1777-8   *Percy* performed at the Covent Garden theatre.

1778   Richard Samuel paints her as one of the "Nine Living
            Muses of Great Britain."

1779   David Garrick dies; More becomes Eva Garrick's
            companion. After the failure of *The Fatal Falsehood*, More
            abandons writing for the stage.

1780   Frances Reynolds paints Hannah's portrait. Hannah begins
            friendship with Horace Walpole. Robert Raikes, newspaper
            editor, founds the Sunday school movement in Gloucester.

1782   Publishes *Sacred Dramas* and *Sensibility: A Poem*.

1783   Writes *The Bas Bleu*, a celebration of Bluestocking culture.
            Jacob More dies.

1784   Begins to correspond with Horace Walpole; befriends Ann
            Yearsley, the "Bristol Milkwoman." Samuel Johnson dies.

1785   Buys Cowslip Green in Somerset; quarrels with Ann Yearsley over a deed of trust.

1786   Mary More (mother) dies.

1787   Meets the former slave trader John Newton, and the abolitionists William Wilberforce and Thomas Clarkson.

1788   Publishes *Slavery: A Poem* and *Thoughts on the Importance of the Manners of the Great to General Society.*

1789   French Revolution begins. Hannah and Patty More found the first of the Mendip schools at Cheddar, Somerset; other schools follow at Shipham, Rowberrow, Nailsea, Blagdon, and Wedmore (also a few more smaller schools).

1791   Publishes *An Estimate of the Religion of the Fashionable World.* John Wesley dies.

1792   Founds women's benefit clubs at Cheddar and Shipham.

1793   In response to Paine's *Rights of Man,* More publishes *Village Politics.* France and Britain are at war. More publishes *Remarks on the Speech of M. Dupont* in aid of the French emigrant clergy.

1795–8   Edits the *Cheap Repository Tracts,* a series of moralist publications based on popular chapbooks and ballads.

1799   Publishes her most important conduct book, *Strictures on the Modern System of Female Education.*

1799–1802   The Blagdon Controversy: one of More's teachers is accused
            of Methodism; the accusation widens into a series of attacks
            on More for alleged religious and political subversion; as a
            result, she suffers depression and a nervous collapse.

1800   Elizabeth Montagu dies.

1801   Builds Barley Wood, her new Somerset home.

1803   Publishes patriotic ballads to encourage her countrymen
            during fears of a French invasion.

1804   Publishes anonymously "The White Slave Trade" in the
            evangelical journal the *Christian Observer,* attacking the
            frivolity of the London fashionable world.

1805   Publishes anonymously *Hints towards Forming the
            Character of a Young Princess* for Princess Charlotte, the
            heiress presumptive to the throne.

1807   The Abolition of the Slave Trade Act passes in Parliament.
            John Newton dies.

1808   Publishes anonymously her only novel, *Coelebs in Search of
            a Wife;* it rapidly becomes a bestseller.

1811   Publishes *Practical Piety.*

1813   Mary More (sister) dies. Hannah supports the campaign,
            launched by Wilberforce, to send Anglican missionaries
            to India; founds an auxiliary Bible Society at Wrington;
            publishes *Christian Morals.*

1814   Samuel Taylor Coleridge visits Barley Wood.

1815   At the Battle of Waterloo, Britain's endless war with France
            is virtually over. More publishes *Essay on the Character and
            Writings of St Paul.*

1816   Elizabeth More (sister) dies.

1817   Sally More (sister) dies. Hannah writes new loyalist tracts
            to counter resurgent radicalism. The death of Princess
            Charlotte creates a succession crisis in Britain.

1819   Patty More (sister) dies. More's loyalist tracts published
            as *Cheap Repository Tracts Suited to the Present Times;*
            publishes *Moral Sketches* and an abolitionist poem,
            The Twelfth of August, or The Feast of Freedom. Birth of
            Princess Victoria.

1821   Publishes *Bible Rhymes* in an attempt to counter religious
            skepticism.

1825   Publishes *The Spirit of Prayer.*

1828   Leaves Barley Wood when told that her servants have been
            cheating her; settles at Clifton, Bristol.

1833   Death of William Wilberforce. More dies at Clifton; buried
            at Wrington, Somerset, near Barley Wood. Oberlin College
            founded, the first college in the world to admit both males
            and females.

1852   Harriet Beecher Stowe publishes *Uncle Tom's Cabin.*

1853   Illinois Institute founded in Wheaton, Illinois, by
           Methodists, later to be renamed Wheaton College in 1860
           under new president Jonathan Blanchard.

British Monarchs during Hannah's Life

House of Hanover

George II	1727–1760
George III	1760–1820
George IV	1820–1830
William IV	1830–1837
(Victoria	1837–1901)

Works by Hannah More

The Search after Happiness: A Pastoral Drama (London, 1773)

The Inflexible Captive: A Tragedy (London, 1774)

Sir Eldred of the Bower and the Bleeding Rock: Two Legendary Tales (Dublin, 1776)

Ode to Dragon, Mr. Garrick's House Dog at Hampton (London, 1777)

Essays on Various Subjects, Principally Designed for Young Ladies (London, 1777)

Percy, A Tragedy (London, 1778)

The Fatal Falsehood: A Tragedy (London, 1779)

Sacred Dramas: Chiefly Intended for Young Persons: The Subjects taken from the Bible. To which is added, Sensibility, a Poem (London, 1782)

Florio: A Tale for Fine Gentlemen and Fine Ladies; and The Bas Blue; or, Conversation: Two Poems (Dublin, 1786)

Slavery: A Poem (London, 1788)

Thoughts on the Manners of the Great to General Society (London, 1788)

Bishop Bonner's Ghost (Twickenham, 1789)

An Estimate of the Religion of the Fashionable World by One of the Laity (London, 1791)

Village Politics Addressed to all the Mechanics, Journeymen and Day Labourers in Great Britain, by Will Cheap, a Country Carpenter (London, 1793)

Remarks on the Speech of M. Dupont, made in the National Convention of France on the Subjects of Religion and Public Education (London, 1793)

Cheap Repository Tracts Published during the Year 1795 (London and Bath)

Cheap Repository Tracts Published during the Year 1796 (London and Bath)

Cheap Repository Tracts, Entertaining Moral and Religious Publications (London, 1798)

Cheap Repository Shorter Tracts (London, 1798)

Cheap Repository Tracts for Sunday Reading (London, 1798)

Strictures on the Modern System of Female Education, with a View of the Principles and Conduct Prevalent among Women of Rank and Fortune, 2 vols. (London, 1799)

The Works of Hannah More in Eight Volumes, including several pieces never before published, 8 vols. (London, 1801)

"The White Slave Trade," Christian Observer, 3 (Mar. 1804), 151-4.

Hints Towards Forming the Character of a Young Princess, 2 vols. (London, 1805)

Cœlebs in Search of a Wife: Comprehending Observations on Domestic Habits, 2 vols. (London, 1809)

Practical Piety: or, The Influence of the Religion of the Heart on the Conduct of the Life, 2 vols. (London, 1811)

Christian Morals, 2 vols. (London, 1813)

An Essay on the Character and Practical Writings of St. Paul, 2 vols. (London, 1815)

The Works of Hannah More: A New Edition, 18 vols. (London, 1818)

Moral Sketches of Prevailing Opinions and Manners, Foreign and Domestic (London, 1820)

The Twelfth of August; or, The Feast of Freedom (London, 1819)

Cheap Repository Tracts Suited to the Present Times (London, 1819)

Bible Rhymes on the Names of All the Books of the Old and New Testament with Allusions to Some of the Principal Incidents and Characters (London, 1821)

The Spirit of Prayer by Hannah More. Selected and Compiled by Her from Various Portions Exclusively on the Subject of Her Published Volumes, 11 vols. (London, 1825)

ACKNOWLEDGMENTS

Readers might wonder, why devote a book to a woman who lived over 250 years ago? I had not heard of Hannah More either until I picked up a copy of *Amazing Grace: William Wilberforce and the Heroic Campaign to End Slavery* by Eric Metaxas (Harper SanFrancisco, 2007). Hannah More, I learned, was pivotal in Wilberforce's campaign, so much so that I googled her to learn more about this unsung heroine of the eighteenth century. I am indebted to Eric Metaxas for introducing me to this intriguing and brilliant woman and to all the others who have chronicled her life, especially Anne Stott.

Stott's well-researched biography, *Hannah More: The First Victorian* (Oxford University Press, 2003) gave me the idea that Hannah's inspiring story as an early abolitionist and philanthropist could capture American readers eager to achieve racial reconciliation and make a difference in the world. Stott also directed me to Mr. Mervyn Harding, who actually lives in More's birth house in Fishponds. Mr. Harding, also intrigued by this Bristol native, volunteered to guide my husband and me to some of the nearby Hannah More villages and school sites on a sunny June day in 2012.

A very special thank-you goes to my valiant husband, Bill, who expertly navigated those narrow backcountry roads as we located the markers that bore witness to the life of this courageous woman. There is nothing like physically exploring the countryside where Hannah More and her sister clopped through on horseback over two hundred years earlier. Bill also helped greatly with photography and research in the libraries of Wheaton College (Illinois), Kenyon College, The Folger Shakespeare Library, The New York Public Library, and the Cambridge University Munby Rare Books Collection. I am deeply grateful to the librarians and archivists in these facilities who assisted me with suggestions and permissions. In addition, I am indebted to Jean and Chris Stephenson for their kind hospitality while visiting Cambridge and to Adrian and Miyoko Thorpe in Sherborne, Dorset, who graciously accommodated us while we investigated the Bristol area.

One of the joys in writing this book was the discovery of the portrait of Hannah More painted by Gilbert Stuart, hanging in the hall of notables at Kenyon College, Gambier, Ohio, and presented in this book with special permission from the Graham Gund Gallery (Julie Leone, Manager). Also, special thanks to Lynn Manner, Carmen King, and Lydia Shahan in Special Collections at Kenyon College.

Lori Loftin, an early, longtime admirer of Hannah More, encouraged me throughout this project. Ms. Loftin actually owns an author-signed, leather-bound volume of Hannah's only novel, *Cœlebs in Search of a Wife*. After instructing me to don white gloves, Lori permitted me to carefully leaf through and admire with delight her precious rare book by Hannah More.

Countless others helped and encouraged me along the way, directly or indirectly: Marjory Lamp Mead, Lisa Richmond, Christine Colón, Wayne Martindale, Mark Noll, Lori Mulligan Davis, Dotsey Welliver, Dennis Hensley, Kenneth Kelling, Karen Swallow Prior, and Greg Johnson. I am also grateful to Wikipedia, the online encyclopedia, for their vast collection of images and portraits in the public domain that flesh out the people of Hannah's world, all before the discovery of photography. All images not attributed are in the public domain.

WORKS CITED
AND CONSULTED

Jonathan Aitkin, *John Newton: From Disgrace to Amazing Grace.* Wheaton, Illinois: Crossway Books, 2007. This book draws attention to Newton's influence on Hannah More through his sermons and writings, which were major factors in changing the course of her life toward Christian service.

Roger Anstey, *The Atlantic Slave Trade and British Abolition 1760–1810.* Atlantic Highlands, New Jersey: Humanities Press, 1975. In this weighty 425-page volume, the Cambridge professor regards the theology of the Quakers and evangelicals as the actual dynamic behind the political process that brought about the abolition of the slave trade in England.

David W. Bebbington, *Evangelicalism in Modern Britain: A History from the 1730s to the 1980s.* London: Unwin Hyman, 1989. This book provides a thorough overview for the background and understanding of evangelicalism and the development of mission agencies.

Ian Bradley, *The Call to Seriousness: The Evangelical Impact on the Victorians.* New York: MacMillan, 1976. With many references to Hannah More, this book details the powerful ways the evangelicals influenced the behavior of people to noble ideals and warned of the dangers of immoral conduct.

Ford K. Brown, *Fathers of the Victorians: The Age of Wilberforce.* Cambridge: Cambridge University Press, 1961. Despite the title, the author gives ample coverage to the literary, philanthropic, educational, and social importance of women like Hannah More and her circle.

Norma Clarke, *Dr. Johnson's Women*. London: Hambledon and London, 2000. This book investigates the lives and writings of six leading female authors of his circle, including Hannah More, and what it was like to be a woman writer in the "Age of Johnson."

Christine A. Colón, *Joanna Baillie and the Art of Moral Influence*. New York: Peter Lang, 2009. This source is useful in tracing the heritage of religious women writers and how women authors who write from an explicitly Christian perspective are often ignored by feminist scholars.

Claire Crogan, "Mary Wollstonecroft and Hannah More: Feminism and Modern Critics," 1994, in *Lumen*, published for the Canadian Society for 18th Century Studies, Vol. XIII, Queens University, Quebec.

Leonore Davidoff and Catherine Hall, *Family Fortunes: Men and Women of the English Middle Class, 1780–1850*. Chicago: University of Chicago Press, 1987. This study, influenced by the Women's Liberation Movement, highlights the role of evangelicals such as William Cowper, Hannah More, and William Wilberforce and their critiques of dissolute behaviors of the aristocratic class.

Donald W. Dayton, *Discovering an Evangelical Heritage*. New York: Harper & Row, 1976. The author highlights the reform movements that sprang from the early evangelicals in England and America. Especially helpful is his groundbreaking chapter on "The Evangelical Roots of Feminism."

Patricia Demers, *The World of Hannah More*. Lexington: University of Kentucky Press, 1996.

By neither idealizing nor demonizing the subject, the author tries to show how biblically inspired principles, royalist sympathies, and a keen observation of social mores guided all of More's work.

Patricia Demers, *Women as Interpreters of the Bible*. New York/Mahwah, N J: Paulist Press, 1992. The author reviews and interprets More's hymns and writings.

John Feather, *A History of British Publishing*. New York: Routledge, 2006.

Jan Fergus, *Jane Austen and the Didactic Novel*. Totowa, NJ: Barnes & Noble Books, 1983. The author speaks of the ways Jane Austen developed her craft in novel writing and the "astringent criticisms" of the society she portrayed.

Charles Howard Ford, *Hannah More: A Critical Biography*. New York: Peter Lang, 1996. In this work, the author seeks to rehabilitate Hannah More from the dim light given her by the feminist social historians who have found her too conservative for their tastes, despite the fact that she was a reformer and not a reactionary in a man's world.

Alice C. C. Gaussen, *A Later Pepys: The Correspondence of Sr. William Weller Pepys, Bart., Master of the Chancery 1758–1825, with Mrs. Chapone, Mrs. Hartley, Mrs. Montagu, Hannah More, and Others*. Edited with an introduction and notes by Alice C.C. Gaussen in two volumes. New York and London: John Lane Publishers, 1904.

William Hague, *William Wilberforce: The Life of the Great Anti-Slave Trade Campaigner*. New York: Harcourt, 2007. The author attests that Wilberforce's friendship with Hannah More was one of the greatest of his life and that it was More who introduced Wilberforce to Charles and John Wesley.

Mary Alden Hopkins, *Hannah More and Her Circle*. New York: Longmans, Green and Co., 1947. A highly readable biography largely based on William Roberts' *Memoirs of the Life and Correspondence of Mrs. Hannah More*.

Echo Irving, *A Brief Life of Hannah More*. Yatton, North Somerset: First Word Services, 2007. Booklet available for purchase to visitors at All Saints' Church, Wrington, North Somerset, where the More sisters are buried in the churchyard.

David Lyle Jeffrey, *English Spirituality in the Age of Wesley*. Grand Rapids, MI: William B. Eerdmans Publishing Company, 1987. This anthology provides an introduction to the general reader with some of the best of English spiritual writing from Watts to Wilberforce, including entries by Hannah More.

Francis A. Knight, *The Heart of Mendip*. London: J. M. Dent & Sons Ltd, 1915. The author gives an account of the history, archeology, and natural history of the parishes of Shipham, Rowberrow, Axbridge, Cheddar, and other towns in the Mendip Hills.

Elizabeth Kowaleski-Wallace, *Their Fathers' Daughters: Hannah More, Maria Edgeworth, and Patriarchal Complicity*. Oxford: Oxford University Press, 1991. The author argues that eighteenth century literary women looked to their fathers for approval and thus perpetuated a patriarchal hierarchy, which was why Hannah More found herself often in the company of accomplished men.

Katelyn E. Ludwig, *Reinventing the Feminine: Bluestocking Women Writers in 18th-Century London*, MA thesis, Emerson College, 2006.

Peter Martin, *Samuel Johnson, a Biography*. Cambridge, MA: Harvard University Press, 2008.

Simon McVeigh, *Concert Life in London from Mozart to Haydn*. Cambridge University Press, 1995. This book analyzes audiences, programs, and venues to describe the musical and cultural life of England's capital city.

Anne K. Mellor, *Mothers of the Nation: Women's Political Writing in England, 1780–1830*. Bloomington, Indiana University Press, 2002. The author argues that women writers, too often dismissed as conservative and retrogressive, "promoted a revolution in cultural mores ." Hannah More, especially, is highlighted for her powerful model in philanthropy that provided a practical model for women of all classes in British society.

Eric Metaxas, *Amazing Grace: William Wilberforce and the Heroic Campaign to End Slavery*. Harper SanFrancisco, 2007. In this biography, the author sheds special light on the role Hannah More played in campaigns to abolish slavery and the reformation of manners.

Sylvia Harcstark Myers, *The Bluestocking Circle: Women, Friendship, and the Life of the Mind in Eighteenth-Century England*. Oxford: Claredon Press, 1990. The author presents the lives and works of women against the prevailing traditions of the time that prevented women from becoming educated and from fullly and actively taking part in intellectual life.

Mark A. Noll, *The Rise of Evangelicalism: The Age of Edwards, Whitefield, and the Wesleys*. Downers Grove, IL: InterVarsity Press, 2003. This book examines where evangelicals came from, what motivated them, and their widespread influence throughout the world in the eighteenth century.

Oxford Dictionary of National Biography, Oxford University Press, 2009.

James Pickering, Jr., *The Moral Tradition in English Fiction, 1785–1850.* Hanover, NH: University Press of New England, 1976. This book explores how the Sunday school movement, Hannah More, and her imitators sought to provide moral instruction to Britons through inexpensive religious tracts.

Karen Irene Swallow Prior, *Hannah More and the Evangelical Contribution to the English Novel,* PhD thesis (Buffalo, NY, 1999). This work emphasizes More's unique position as a bridge between the social, religious, economic, and cultural chasms that defined eighteenth-century English society.

Peter Quennell, *Samuel Johnson: His Friends and Enemies.* New York: American Heritage Press, 1973. Hannah More was, of course, one of Samuel Johnson's friends; this book, with its many photographs and illustrations, provides a look at the background of their social period.

George A. Rawlyk and Mark A. Noll, eds., *Amazing Grace: Evangelicalism in Australia, Britain, Canada, and the United States.* Grand Rapids: Baker Books, 1993. Ted A. Campbell's essay in particular highlights the role of Hannah More's influential writings, which spanned the Atlantic and were enthusiastically received in the early American republic.

Arthur Roberts, ed., *Mendip Annals: or a Narrative of the Charitable Labours of Hannah and Martha More in Their Neighbourhood, being the Journal of Martha More.* New York: Robert Carter & Brothers, 1859. This 253-page treasure is dedicated to "the Lady Olivia Bernard Sparrow, the valued friend and correspondent of Hannah More, and, like her a helper of the truth as it is in Jesus." A first-person history concerning the schools founded in the villages in the Mendip Hills, this charming book adds excerpts from letters heretofore unpublished from William Wilberforce and Hannah More.

William Roberts, *Memoirs of the Life and Correspondence of Hannah More,* 4 vols. London: R. B. Seely and Sons, 1834. Out of print but available online, this book was compiled from hundreds of letters bequeathed to Roberts's sister Margaret Roberts, Hannah More's literary executor.

Mona Scheuermann, *In Praise of Poverty: Hannah More Counters Thomas Paine and the Radical Threat.* Lexington: University of Kentucky Press, 2002. The author's purpose is to show that Hannah More's writings represented "the beliefs and fear of her peers as they encountered the social order—and the threat of disorder— in the 1790s and the years following."

Mary Anne Schofield and Cecilia Macheski, eds., *Fettered or Free? British Women Novelists, 1670–1850.* Athens, OH: Ohio University Press, 1986. Mitzi Myers's entry, "Hannah More's Tracts for the Times: Social Fiction and Female Ideology," gives prime examples of Hannah More tackling social and cultural issues of her day.

M.K. Smith, "Hannah More: Sunday schools, education and youth work," *The Encyclopedia of Informal Education* (2002), www.infed.org/thinkers/more.htm.

Jane Spencer, *The Rise of the Woman Novelist from Aphra Behn to Jane Austen.* Oxford: Basil Blackwell, 1986. This book considers the attitudes toward women's writing, the traditions of didacticism and romance in women's fiction, and women writers' search for acceptance.

Rodney Stark, *For the Glory of God: How Monotheism Led to Reformations, Science, Witch-hunts, and the End of Slavery.* Princeton: Princeton

University Press, 2003. Although this book by a sociologist does not mention Hannah More, its overall purpose is to show how ideas about God have shaped the history and culture of the West and therefore the world.

Anne Stott, *Hannah More: The First Victorian*. Oxford: Oxford University Press, 2003. This thorough and informative biography includes many helpful maps, illustrations, and the Hannah More chronology used in this book that aids the reader in following More's many achievements.

Thomas Taylor, *Memoir of Hannah More with Notices of Her Works and Sketches of Her Contemporaries*. London: Joseph Rickerby, Printer, Sherbourn Lane, 1838. The author states that he endeavored to give (in 423 pages) a "brief, yet complete and faithful detail of Mrs. More's life . . . and to trace the steady growth of her Christian character . . . amidst the most vexatious hostility."

Henry Thompson, *The Life of Hannah More*. London: Cadell, 1838. The author was a curate who came to Wrington, Somerset, after Hannah's death and draws heavily from people who knew her when she was alive.

Ruth A. Tucker and Walter L. Liefeld. *Daughters of the Church: Women and Ministry from New Testament Times to the Present*. Grand Rapids, MI: Academie Books, 1987. The authors have highlighted the prominent role of women in major movements, including Hannah More and her significant contribution in fostering schools among the poor.

John Wolffe, *The Expansion of Evangelicalism: The Age of Wilberforce, More, Chalmers, and Finney*. Downers Grove, IL: InterVarsity Press, 2007. This book underscores Hannah More as not only a highly influential writer but also a "role model for activist evangelical women."

Yonge, Charlotte M, *Hannah More*. London: W.H. Allen & Co., 1888. This 198-page biography was part of the *Eminent Women Series,* edited by John H. Engram, that already included George Eliot, Emily Brontë, Mary Wollstonecraft Godwin, and Susanna Wesley, among others.

INDEX

Page numbers in **bold** indicate text accompanied by illustrations.

Connect with the author:
www.MaryAnnePhemister.com